Roger and Donna
We wanted you to have a copy of our book and trust it will be a blessing and inspire you to a greater level of trust and faith. Knowing our God will never fail you in the present and future perilous times. We know with our God the best is yet to come. Let us know what you think of the book?

1 Thess 1: 2+3　　*1 Chron 4:10*

Secrets to Our
Supernatural Walk with God

D1706694

Howard and Betty Skinner

Howard and Betty Skinner

6-27-11

970-377-8329

WestBow
PRESS
A DIVISION OF THOMAS NELSON

WestBow Press books may be ordered through booksellers or by contacting:

WestBow Press
A Division of Thomas Nelson
1663 Liberty Drive
Bloomington, IN 47403
www.westbowpress.com
1-(866) 928-1240

Because of the dynamic nature of the Internet, any web addresses or links contained in this book may have changed since publication and may no longer be valid. The views expressed in this work are solely those of the author and do not necessarily reflect the views of the publisher, and the publisher hereby disclaims any responsibility for them.

Any people depicted in stock imagery provided by Thinkstock are models, and such images are being used for illustrative purposes only.

Certain stock imagery © Thinkstock.

ISBN: 978-1-4497-1733-9 (sc)
ISBN: 978-1-4497-1732-2 (hc)
ISBN: 978-1-4497-1731-5 (e)

Library of Congress Control Number: 2011928731

Printed in the United States of America

WestBow Press rev. date: 05/18/2011

This book is an autobiography of a man who went from a lying prisoner as a boy to a liberated preacher of truth and faith. This story will compel you to trust God in the midst of hardship and trial. God used this man around the world to encourage, strengthen and edify the church. You will be inspired by its truth and challenged to believe God through impossible circumstances.

Dary Northrop
Lead Pastor of Timberline Church
Fort Collins, CO

Here is the story of a man of God who has sought to take God at His Word and experience a life of ministry characterized by signs and wonders. His story is interesting, faith-building and designed to strengthen the body of Christ. You are invited to take the journey with Howard and Betty Skinner as they together have sought to follow the leading of the Holy Spirit in ministry around the world.

Richard L. Dresselhaus
Former Pastor
San Diego First Assembly of God

Howard Skinner is an inspiration! In the time I have known Howard, I have come to respect and admire his openness, honesty, and character which he demonstrates on a daily basis. As a pastor and itinerant preacher, Howard has truly walked the walk and talked the talk in decades of ministry. His love and honor for His Savior permeates his life, and therefore, his book. I believe the prophetic gifting which is so apparent in his life is truly reflected in the last chapter as he encourages believers to be strong and courageous as end of the age approaches. It is a privilege for me to endorse this book; I have been personally blessed by this man of God and know you will too.

Jonathan Wiggins
Senior Pastor of Resurrection Fellowship Church
Loveland, Colorado

I have had the honor of knowing Rev. Howard Skinner and his wonderful wife Betty for over thirty years. He has impressed me in so many ways, but two things stand out above the rest. Howard always lives by the Word of God, and he is always led by the Spirit. His life has had him preaching as well as 'doing' the Word. Once, while preaching at our church, he told a childless couple that in one year's time, they would have a child. Of course, they were thrilled when they had a baby boy that year.

As you read this book, you'll see how Howard's dedication to the Word of God and his leadership of the Holy Spirit has touched many pastors and congregations, and it will touch your life, too.

Thank you, Howard, for what you've taught me and for what you and Betty mean to my family and church

Dr. Andre R. Olson
Pastor, Abundant Life Church
Waynesboro; Waynesboro, Mississippi

My acquaintance and friendship with Howard Skinner reaches back more than four decades. I have known Howard to be a man of great faith and daring trust and sensitivity to God's direction in his life and ministry. This personal testimony and record of the remarkable ministry of a man and his devoted wife will inspire the faith of the reader. Read and rejoice with Howard and Betty in the miraculous.

Everett Stenhouse
Former Southern California district superintendent
and retired general counsel, assistant general superintendent

DEDICATION

This book is dedicated to our great GOD, the creator of the heavens and the earth, ABBA FATHER, our faithful father, who loves us and has made every provision for us! To our wonderful Savior the LORD JESUS CHRIST who gave His life on Calvary and has made all things possible to us and for us and has shed His blood and provided for every need that we have. To our precious HOLY SPIRIT who lives within us, who is our leader, our teacher and our guide - who directs us in the paths of righteousness. We dedicate this book and give all the glory to God for all that He has done. We pray that others will come to know Him as their God, their Lord and Savior.

Howard Skinner

Contents

Forward

Howard and Betty Skinner are two of the most precious people I have ever met. They have a deep faith that causes them to truly believe that nothing is impossible with God. Their zeal for God and their deep faith is so strong that it is contagious.

This book reveals how they came to have such faith. Their faith was forged in the fires of adversity where many times a miracle was necessary for survival. Over and over God proved Himself to be faithful to them and as a result, they became risk takers. They truly believed that they could do anything God told them to do!

This book allows each of us to journey with them across the nation and around the globe as they experience the supernatural. As you read it you will find your own faith growing deeper and deeper. The supernatural will begin to seem natural and God will come alive for you in a new way.

Truly, this is a faith building book.

Pastor John Stocker
Pastor Emeritus of Resurrection Fellowship, Loveland CO

Acknowledgments

❦

Thank you Rhonda Kanning Anderson! For many years I had asked the Lord to send someone into my life who had the skillful expertise to help me express our lives and ministry in writing. Rhonda encouraged and inspired me – she believed, without wavering, that our stories and secrets of walking supernaturally must be in print. Her positive vision and keen perception has been an inspiration to me as we persevered. I am grateful for Rhonda's commitment and her effort that has guided me through this process from transcribing audio-cassette tapes all the way to the publication of this book.

I also want to thank Mick Diener, Laura Harbolt and Greg Skoog who gave their precious time and energy assisting in editorial laboring. Their gifts enabled us to retain the flavor of my intent and originality. I know that this message of walking supernaturally and the personal prophetic intensity written in this manuscript is without contradiction and is relevant for these last days.

Genuine thanks to all who have prayed for us through the years and likewise for those who have given us words and encouragement to write this book.

Thanks to my wife, sweetheart and lifelong companion, Betty. She had a burning passion for the completion of this book. I am thankful for her inspiration, prayers, patience and partnership with this project.

She generously spent innumerable hours editing and proof reading my work in addition to writing her own chapters.

We are extremely grateful to our parents, Isaac and Violette Skinner and Cecil and Mary Lorraine Enochs, whom have all gone to their eternal reward. They faithfully served the Lord and enriched our lives with this beautiful Pentecostal heritage.

We thank our daughters and their spouses, our two grandsons and their wives and our two great granddaughters. They inspire us with their love and their steadfast determination to continue carrying the torch of the Holy Spirit which is their heritage.

Howard Skinner

INTRODUCTION

⁂

This book has been in the making for a lifetime. In the late 70's, and up to the present time, I began to receive prophesies that I should write a book. I suppose there have been many dozens of this identical prophesy, but I felt in my heart, the writing of this book must be written according to God's perfect plan and timing. I had no desire to write a book just for the sake of being an author. My purpose for writing this book is for no personal fame or gain but to bring glory to His name. I pray it will encourage the body of Christ to believe God no matter how dark it looks. He will provide and bring you through for Jesus will do what He said He will do. We share our experiences so that you may be inspired to have faith to believe God to work in your life even as we have experienced in our own lives. We believe the Lord will take what we say and inspire you to believe Him and rise up in faith.

The purpose of this book is also to help you know that God will keep His Word and all things work together for good to those who love the Lord and are called according to His purpose. If you will trust in the Lord with all your heart, with all your soul, with all your mind and all your strength and lean not to your own understanding, the Lord surely will bring to pass His promises in your life. We seek to lift up the Lord Jesus Christ and relate these experiences that demonstrate how He has been faithful as we have exercised faith in Him. Our little mustard seed faith in a GREAT BIG GOD will bring us into victory every time. So I trust you will take these words and let them burn in your soul as you read every chapter and know that the Lord will meet your needs as He has met ours. We allowed the Lord Jesus Christ to take control of our circumstances and meet every need, for we were never to ask for money or solicit funds. This is the way God led us, for we were never to ask for a meeting, but God has taken us all around the world and abundantly supplied our needs. So it is with this prayer as you read this book that you will have faith for the future, because we need to FEARLESSLY FACE THE FUTURE IN FAITH for there are difficult days coming and the Lord Jesus wants us to know that He is trustworthy and faithful. He will teach us how to walk the supernatural walk of faith with Him. I pray as you read this book, your heart will be stirred to know that God will see you through and He will bring forth His plan for your life as you hold steadfast and always trust in Him. I pray this book will touch the Body of Christ and you who don't know Jesus will accept Him as your Savior and Lord knowing that He is a good God and will surely forgive anyone of their sins who come to Him! The desire that is in our hearts is to lift up Jesus. But you must put your faith in action for He is a miracle worker. "All things are possible to him that believeth." Faith that has not works is dead, so trust in the Lord and move forward in His name. Surely God will bring to pass all that He has planned for your life.

CHAPTER ONE

❦

A Hook in My Jaw

March 25, 1929 – I was the first born of six boys. I was a hydrocephalic child which, in layman's terms, means that I was a water-head baby. I also had yellow jaundice and my parents, Isaac and Violette Skinner, tell me the crown of my head was down to the back of my neck. My parents had been saved only a year before I was born and were attending a Full Gospel church in Grand Island, Nebraska. It was quite a drive from the small town of Harvard, where I was born, but as often as they could, they would go. And that is where they took me, to be prayed for.

Dr. Pelz said they should just pray that God would take this child because his head would become so large and so heavy he would not be able to move and would surely die anyway. But my parents never waivered in their faith that God would heal their baby boy.

As Pastor White from the church in Grand Island began to pray, and the church prayed with him, almost instantly, liquid began to discharge from my ear. Within a few days my head was of normal size and in the proper place. A few weeks later my parents were able to go back to church and I was dedicated to the Lord. The pastor held me up and prophesied that God was going to use this child in a marvelous way.

Later my parents moved to Hastings, Nebraska, where they helped pioneer a Full Gospel church. It was there, at the age of about five or six, I gave my life to the Lord. I remember lying on the sawdust floor, weeping, and asking Jesus to come into my heart. I was filled with the Holy Spirit, speaking with other tongues, and I felt assured that I was called to the ministry.

Even before then, when I was about four or five years old, I would try to preach. I remember setting up tin cans, fruit jars and rocks. I would take a wooden apple box out under the oak tree where we lived and pound my fist and cry "Send the power!" As far back as I can remember, the power of the Spirit has been in my life, along with the call and the desire to preach the gospel.

The 1930s were very difficult times. But we loved the Lord and went to church regularly. We loved God even through the years of the dust bowl, when dust would pile up as if it were snow drifting around our house, and when the plague of grasshoppers swooped down and devoured everything green before our eyes. We had to adjust during these very trying years,. But we had confidence that God was with us, for we learned to totally trust Him.

At church, our Revivals lasted night after night - we would wear out one Evangelist and then start with another one. Some services ended before midnight and my parents were very concerned that we were backsliding and were going the way of the other church denominations. But God continued to bless and move in our hearts and our lives. We trusted Him and He proved faithful through those trying depression years.

At about the age of 15, I began to draw back from the Lord as I had become very concerned with the call to preach. To be honest, I really didn't believe that I could preach, or that I was worthy, or that I was capable. In fact, during public school, I wouldn't even give a book report. I would rather take an "F" in that particular subject than speak before a crowd. So I began to pull away from the Lord and the church.

I found a job at the Burlington Railroad in Lincoln, icing refrigerator cars. I worked the midnight shift and one night, before I went to work, I was in a rebellion session against my parents. My Dad said to me, "Son, God will take care of you and His hand is on your life, for I know you're going to be a preacher and somehow God will cause it to come to pass." I left for work, slammed the door, but remembered the words my Dad said. God would take care of me.

At work that evening, my job was to spot huge cubes of ice to put in the refrigerator cars. To do this I had to be 20 feet in the air on an ice dock as the conveyor brought the 300-pound cakes of ice. I had what we called a pike pole and was pushing the ice into place for the arriving refrigerator cars. As the cubes of ice were coming up the conveyor belt, I started falling behind, so I began to hurry.

I stabbed the pike pole into the ice to remove it from the conveyor chain. A pike pole has a hook on one end and a point on the other to push the ice wherever you want it to go. But the pole kept slipping, and I was getting excited and trying to catch up. I tried again and my pike pole slipped once more. Then I hurriedly hooked one more time, yanking with all my might. But the pike pole slipped and I felt myself tumbling off the ice dock backwards, landing on the railroad tracks in the shipyard.

I fell 20 feet from the dock, resulting in a broken back, a broken tailbone, a smashed hip and kidneys that wouldn't function. I was really in bad shape and wondered if I was going to live.

While lying there in the hospital bed, I began to remember the words of my father saying, "Son, God will take care of you and His hand is on your life, for I know you're going to be a preacher and somehow God will cause it to come to pass." I knew at that moment that the Lord had a hook in my jaw and wasn't going to let me go. But, like those stubborn blocks of ice, I became more determined I was going to go my way. I was convinced I could not preach. I just knew I could not stand before people to speak or minister. So I hardened my heart more.

My parents sent the pastor to pray for me, but I was firmly resolved to go my way. And yet the Lord miraculously and supernaturally healed me, through His mercy and His grace, and I walked out of the hospital within 30 days.

The doctors told me that I shouldn't do any hard, physical labor for some time, though my past occupations had always demanded physical labor. I had always worked – since I was about six. When I was a little boy I started a candy bar route during the heart of the Depression. I would buy candy bars, three for a dime, and sell them for a nickel apiece. I believe I was the first full-gospel businessman! I established a route and, in the beginning, made 35-45 cents every day after school until I was about 12. Then I worked in a grocery store for about three and a half years, after school and on Saturdays. As a child, I always had some kind of work and bought all my own clothes.

Now, not being able to do physical labor, I found a job with a magazine crew, who were selling magazines and traveling to different states. Later, one of the fellows from the magazine crew said, "I know a way we can make money a lot easier and make more of it. He explained how you could sell a prayer card, acting as deaf mute. He mentioned he had done this before and made up to $100 a day. That was a lot of money in 1947. He explained that you have a prayer printed on a card which says, "Lord, help us to preserve the peace that so many have suffered and died to gain."

Then you use another small business card that says, "Dear friend, being handicapped by deafness and unable to speak, I'm selling this prayer itself for 25 cents. Please pay what you wish." The plan was to go to business places, to bars or restaurants and lay down both cards to all the customers; then go back and gather the money. The fellow said that sometimes people would give you a dollar and he reconfirmed you could easily make $100 a day.

This sounded very enticing to me. So I joined the fellow. There were days when I did make $100 and would have money running out my pockets. For quite some time this financial situation was going well and I said to myself, "I'm making more money than I have ever made in my life and I don't have to **say a word!**"

So I began to make bigger plans for myself; taking on the attitude of the rich young fool in the 12th chapter of Luke. The man became very prosperous and said, "I don't have enough room to contain all of the goods that I have, so I'm going to build bigger barns and I'm going to really prosper and be great. I will say to my soul, thou hast much goods laid up for many years; take thy ease, eat, drink and be merry."

Then God said, "Thou fool, this night thy soul shall be required of thee, then whose shall those things be which thou hast provided."

But God was not a part of my plans! One day the man who had taught me how to sell the prayer cards as a deaf mute went to Plattsmouth, Nebraska, and I went to Glenwood, Iowa. The towns were about 7 miles apart, just across the state line. I went into a drugstore to sell the prayer cards and as I was presenting them to different customers in the store, the owner of the store came up and began to talk to me in sign language.

Of course, I didn't know sign language, so I wrote on a pad and told him that I didn't know sign language. I didn't know it at the time, but his parents were deaf mutes and he immediately became very suspicious of me and called the police.

The police came and took me to the police station and began to interrogate me. After several hours of trying to get me to talk to them, they were just nearly ready to give up, concluding I was either a deaf mute or I was the best actor they had ever seen. For a period of time, two or three policemen would look directly at me while another policeman would creep up behind me. He would suddenly scream and the policemen in front would watch my eyes to see if I blinked.

I was quite the actor and it sounded like they were about ready to let me go when one of the officers found a phone number in my wallet with a Lincoln area code. So he put me in a squad car to go back to the state line. He meant to try getting in touch with someone who knew something about me, using the number he found. That phone number belonged to my grandmother, whom I had stopped to see that morning.

Using their police radio, they contacted the police in Lincoln, who got in touch with my grandmother. They asked her if I was a deaf mute.

Of course she told them, "No, he was here this morning and he was all right." I was nabbed for sure.

But I still refused to talk, so they took me back to the police station and interrogated me again. They tracked down my parents and told me they were on the way and would arrive the next day. I could see no way out. I finally looked up and said, "Yes, I can talk!"

That was a **life-altering day**, for my plans were going to change, and God's purposes and plans were about to be set in motion. Jeremiah 29:11 tells us, "For I know the thoughts and the plans that I have for you, says the Lord, thoughts and plans for welfare and peace and not for evil, to give you hope in your final outcome."

I was sentenced to six months in the county jail in Glenwood, Iowa. I understand nowadays this offense is just a misdemeanor and requires no sentence. However, at that time, Iowa law said I could have been sentenced to seven years. God had a plan and He had a hook in my jaw that would not let me go. Vernon, the other man who was working in Plattsmouth, Nebraska, also was taken into custody. But the maximum sentence they could give him in Nebraska was 10 days in the county jail, even though he had been selling prayer cards under false pretences for five or six years. Thank God, I was in Iowa. I believe a short, 10-day sentence would have just made me more determined that I could be a tremendous success in this moneymaking business.

While I was in Glenwood, serving my six months, God began to speak to me about getting my life back in line with His plans. At first I was resistant. But He continued to make me miserable in my soul and was calling me back into relationship with Him. I was in this small town jail, all alone most of the time; it was like solitary confinement. But eventually a friend brought me a radio.

On November 30, 1947, I was going across the dial on that radio, searching for something that interested me, when I came onto a preacher. I certainly didn't want to listen to a preacher, so I attempted to turn the dial. To my amazement, I couldn't turn it!

Immediately in my soul, God's Spirit began to work. For at that moment my knees buckled down to the floor and I began to cry out to

God to forgive me and come into my heart. On November 30, 1947, at about 9 in the evening, I turned my life totally, completely over to the Lord.

Even though I didn't think I could preach. Even though I didn't feel capable and I didn't feel worthy, I said, "I'll do whatever you tell me to do, go wherever you tell me to go. **Here I am, Lord!**"

A few days later I was refilled with the Holy Spirit, spoke with other tongues and was recalled into the ministry. From that date to this, my face has been set like flint toward the will of God. All that really matters to me is to someday hear Him say, "Well done, thou good and faithful servant." I am so happy my plan failed and God's plan prevailed.

Since that night, I have pastored eight churches in Indiana, Michigan and California and was an associate pastor in a Baptist church. The Lord has taken me and my wife around the world, ministering in most of our 50 states and in 27 countries. We have never solicited funds or asked for offerings. We've never asked for meetings and yet God opens all the doors through which He wants to send us.

I encourage you to believe God and know that when He gives a vision, there is provision. When He calls you to do something, He will give you the ability to accomplish His purpose. It is still hard for me to believe that God has enabled me to preach the gospel for 62 years.

Philippians 4:13 says, "I can do all things through Christ which strengthens me." This is the main Scripture that I took hold of during the six months that I was shut away. I read the Bible through two and a half times during that time. As I was seeking God, fasting and praying, I'd say to God, "If you have called me to preach the gospel, you're going to help me and you're going to enable me even though I don't feel like I'm qualified."

This began a relationship with the Lord Jesus Christ that I pursue to this day. I had many great experiences in the presence of the Lord during that period of time as I began to study the Word of God and prepare myself for the ministry for which He called me. I had said an eternal yes to God and His will for my life. Thank God for a praying dad and mom! I can remember hearing my dad pray for me in the middle of the night. The Lord gave my dad a word that within six months I would be back in right relationship with God. I always wondered about that phrase in Dad's word from the Lord, "within six months," because that's exactly how long I was confined and was shut in with God.

Chapter Two

A Full-Time Ministry

It was during this period of time that I became very established and intimate with Him. Now that the Lord had me headed in the right direction, I went back to my hometown in Hastings, Nebraska. Our church there was in the middle of a revival meeting, so I went every night to the meetings and during the days I would try to find a job. I borrowed a trailer and went door-to-door, asking if I could haul trash or ashes to the dump. Eventually I got a job at a sandpit for a few months before obtaining a steady job at Western Land Roller, where they made farm equipment.

During all this time, I was very involved in the church. Almost every Saturday, I would meet with the pastor and I would go with him as he made calls on members who had been absent. During our time together I would talk to him about the ministry, for his wise counsel to me was a gift from God.

One day as we were talking he said to me, "So you want to be a preacher? The way you start is to take this dust rag and a broom and go out and clean the bus to prepare for the street meeting we're going to have this evening." About once a week during the summer, a busload from our church would go to a neighboring town to conduct a street meeting. The group would sing, witness and testify to those who would gather around, concluding with a message from the pastor.

That summer, I would go to the church's basement auditorium every evening after work and stay for about three hours. I would be in the presence of the Lord in prayer, praise, worship and Bible study. Many of the young people from the church had other plans for their evenings. And often they would ask me to join them. I told them no, I was going to the church to pray and study the word of God every evening. One by one, the young people began coming to the church and joining me. Soon, quite a group came every evening, even though there wasn't a regular service. Consequently, the young people began to develop a great hunger and thirst after God. One night the pastor came over, as he lived next door. He was so heartened and encouraged to see what was going on. "If you continue this way," he beamed, "it will bring great revival to the church."

It was the summer of 1948 when I preached my first sermon at my home church. I was still very nervous about getting up before a crowd. But God helped me and I was determined that I would do the will of God, knowing He would enable me. In the past, when my parents were gone and left me in charge of babysitting my brothers, I would bring them together; line up the dining room chairs and say, "We're going to have church!" They weren't usually very happy about it. They were even less happy when I made them sing. But I would preach, for it was always in my heart to preach the Gospel. My parents said I would even get behind the radio and act like I was a radio preacher!

But this was the real thing. Each week I faced my fears, stood up and wondered at the way God was causing my future to unfold.

In early September, a group of young people came to our church representing North-Central Theological Seminary in Minneapolis. They sang, gave testimonies and ministered the Word. Their main purpose was to encourage young people to consider going to their school. I prayed earnestly about it, talked to my pastor and to my parents and, within two or three weeks, I was on my way by bus to Minnesota.

At the time, all of my belongings fit into one suitcase. I had very little money but I went to the thrift store and bought a couple of suits, because I understood you had to wear suits at the Bible college.

Still I believed I was walking in the plan of God even though I had very little money or belongings. In Luke 9:3, Jesus said to the disciples, "Take nothing for your journey, neither staves nor script, neither bread nor money, neither have two coats." I felt I was better off than the disciples, for I had a gleam in my eye and a spring in my step knowing that He would never leave me, forsake me or let me down. I was on a journey with Jesus! At that time I had no idea what was ahead and I wondered how God's plan could ever come to pass. I began to learn what it was to truly trust in the Lord.

School had already been in session for about two weeks and they required me to get caught up with the classes. Plus, I needed to find a job right away. Arriving at school late put me at a disadvantage because most of the good jobs near the school were taken. Thankfully, I found a job at a Texaco station where I would service cars.

My job required me to travel about 15 miles by bus across town. In addition, I had to work seven hours a day. School hours were from 8 a.m. till noon and my designated hours for work were from 1 until 8. That year at Bible college was one of the most challenging of my life. Starting school late put me behind and it seemed I could never catch up on my class work. Living alone and paying for school in a strange city meant I needed money. And it seemed I could never quite make enough.

Besides going to school and working seven hours at the Texaco station, for some three months I worked at a restaurant called The Grill, which was about two blocks from the school. I would open the restaurant at 5 a.m., and work until about 10 minutes to 8. Then I would dash out the door and run to my first class.

I was exhausted and couldn't keep up the schedule. So while I did keep up with my work hours, during the last couple of months I started skipping some of my classes. Eventually I had to drop out before the end of the school year. However, I was determined that next year I would do better. I planned to work very hard and long hours in the summer and hold down two jobs if necessary.

If I stuck to it, I could get my school bill all paid up and also be able to pay the school for most of the next year's tuition. It all seemed so possible.

Unfortunately, my boss sold the Texaco station about a month before the new school year was to begin and I lost my job. I began to pray, "Lord, do you have other plans? What do you want me to do?" My parents and family had moved to California, so I had no reason to go back to Nebraska. A friend of mine, who was a graduate of the school was going back home to Kokomo, Indiana. "Come with me," he said. "You can get a job, make money for next year and then return to school."

I often say that I went to Indiana deer hunting and oh, what a dear I found. Betty Lou Enochs was sitting on her Poppa's piano stool, playing the piano. Her father and mother, Cecil and Lorraine Enochs, were pastors of a church in that city. I played the guitar in the services, and when we played certain songs, I had to look to the pianist for the key. I had a tough time looking away.

While Betty technically had a boyfriend, she was only allowed to participate in group dating. Though she was 17, Betty's parents hadn't let her go on a single date. I didn't know this, so one night after church I asked her if I could take her home. She said, "I'll have to ask my father." So she got his permission and I took her home after church.

Betty and I sat out in front of her house for about three hours as I went over my life's history. I told her how God had arrested me and how I had made a total surrender to the Lordship of Jesus Christ. I told her the Lord had called me into the ministry and that I intended to fulfill that call with absolutely nothing hindering me. I really felt like this girl was going to be my wife and I needed to let her know exactly where I stood with the Lord Jesus Christ. If there was any resistance to what I was saying, I decided I wouldn't ask her out anymore because I didn't want to get emotionally involved. I didn't sense any resistance to what I was saying. As a matter of fact, I felt she was agreeing with me. It's a wonder her mother and father didn't come out to the car, where we sat till about midnight. I don't believe she'd ever been out that late before.

We began to date regularly, which mainly meant I took Betty home after church services and rallies in different cities. Six months later, I asked her to marry me and gave her an engagement ring on her 18th birthday, April 28, 1950. We fell more and more in love and set the date for October 1, 1950. All this time we were active in the local church where her father was the pastor. I was the treasurer of the church and we both worked in various departments of the church. We would also minister in various churches. She played the accordion and I played the guitar; we sang together and I would preach the gospel. We knew that together, we were headed for full-time ministry.

On Sunday, October 1, 1950, at three o'clock in the afternoon, we were married. We both seemed to have the same love and commitment to the Lord Jesus Christ and to one another. Even though our marriage was planned for Sunday afternoon, we both went to Sunday school at 9 a.m. and attended morning service. We were married that afternoon and went to the evening youth service at 6 p.m., and the regular 7 p.m. service. This is something we felt in our hearts that we wanted to do. I have to admit I didn't get too much out of the services at night, for I was remembering my beautiful bride walking down the aisle that afternoon and how God had blessed me! I was remembering holding her hand at the wedding and singing, "God gave you to me sweetheart, to make my sky more blue."

It doesn't seem possible that was 60 years ago! We made a covenant together that we would "Seek first the kingdom of God and his righteousness and all these things would be added unto us" as it states in Matthew 6:33.

The next morning we both went to work. I worked at the Chrysler plant and Betty worked then at the 5 & 10 store. Later, she found a job at the Delco plant where they made radios for cars. During our first year of marriage we remained active in our home church in Kokomo. Periodically we would go out and minister, singing and preaching as the Lord opened doors. Soon we were invited to be pastors of a church south of Indianapolis. But neither of us felt that was God's will for us at that time.

About six or seven months after we were married, we met a pastor at a camp meeting. This man was from Gary, Indiana, where he was trying to start a church. He invited us to come and help him by holding a weeklong meeting – Sunday through Sunday. It was early fall when we arrived at the pastor's home where we were to stay during the meeting. They had five children; their ages were from about 5 to 12 years. As I recall, we were to sleep in the children's room and they were to sleep on the floor or on the couch. There was no door to our bedroom, just a drape that was hung across the doorway. They all took turns pushing the curtain aside a bit and peeking in; giggling at us as we were lying in bed. They would come in and out of our room to get things they wanted, but mostly because they were inquisitive. I don't think they ever had anyone staying in their room before; but we loved them and tried to understand that we were imposers in their room as far as they were concerned.

We felt blessed that the Lord opened the door for us to minister for Him. Every one of our services was greatly blessed by the Lord! The pastor lived in Whiting, Indiana, and the church was located in the west part of Gary, which was about 20 or 25 miles away. They were having meetings in a little single-car garage, which had seating capacity for about 50 people. They had an old piano, but I don't believe anyone could play it for it was terribly out of tune. Betty would play her accordion and I would play my guitar, leading them in worship. The few people who were coming to the services began to invite others as they saw God was really blessing the people there. People were being filled with the Spirit and healed.

One night a woman was filled with the Holy Spirit and she was so blessed that she kept speaking in tongues until well after midnight. Finally her husband and another woman picked her up while she was still speaking in other tongues. They put her in the car and her husband said he took her home and had to put her to bed. When he fell off to sleep she was still speaking in her new heavenly language, so he was not sure when she went to sleep. She, her husband and family became great pillars in the church.

When we left that series of meetings to go back to Kokomo, we were rejoicing and praising God for what He had done in saving souls, healing sick bodies, delivering folks from bondage and also for the great refreshing we received in our own souls. God had done great things in that small gathering of people.

A few weeks later I received a call from the pastor in Gary, saying he was closing the church and moving to Arizona. He wanted to know if I would be interested in keeping the church open. I paused and prayed and quickly realized I already knew the Lord had let us know He was sending us there to establish the church body and build a church building. We both felt that calling, so our answer was yes. Betty and I gave two weeks' notice to our employers and set out to follow the Lord's will. It was a great step of faith, for we both had jobs that paid well. And during the year we were married we had paid for our furniture and acquired a better car. But we had very little savings.

Still, we clung to Matthew 6:33, "Seek ye first the kingdom of God and His righteousness and all these things will be added to you." And to Philippians 4:19, "But my God shall supply all your needs according to His riches in glory by Christ Jesus."

In December 1951, we arrived in Gary with a rented four-wheel trailer containing all of our belongings. We proceeded down Colfax Street and pulled around to the back of the house to the chicken coop which would be our new home. The man who was helping me unload the furniture looked at the trailer and then at the chicken coop and told me we would never get it all in. I told him to wait and see. And we did.

All except the washing machine and gas range, which we were able to store in the basement of our landlord who lived in the front house. I never said our house was crowded, just cozy - for we were happy, excited and challenged with our assignment from the Lord.

CHAPTER THREE

❦

Faith Will Build a Church

W e had no idea what God had in store for us, but we knew that He had sent us to Gary. We were standing on His word to us in Jeremiah 1:7, "I will send you where I want you to go and put my word in your mouth." Like Jeremiah, I had no ordination papers or license to preach. But just as He sent Jeremiah, He was sending me. We were starting on our supernatural journey with the Lord with His instructions to establish the body and build the church building. I was only 22 years old and my wife was 19. We had never pastored a church and I knew nothing about building. But we simply believed Him and had no doubt He would help accomplish what He sent us to do.

We were so excited about our first Sunday morning service. We could hardly wait to get to the little garage building with the 49 old folding chairs, the old upright Victrola for my pulpit, the old out-of-tune piano and the little coal-fired stove in the back.

Eleven people showed up for the first service. I played the guitar and Betty played the accordion. We sang, preached the gospel and declared God had sent us there to establish a church body and to build a church building. We agreed that out of the offerings, we would first pay all of the church bills and the remaining balance would go toward living expenses for Betty and me. We told those who attended that we were not going to seek other employment, for we intended to live by faith, fully trusting God to meet every need. We knew God would not fail! Each following Sunday morning we had Sunday school at 9:30 a.m., with the morning worship service following at 10:30. Sunday and Thursday evening services were at 7.

Almost immediately I began to pray and look for a place where we could build a church building. After a few weeks we were regularly having 30 to 35 in our services and I asked the people to earnestly pray that God would lead us to a place where we could build a church.

A woman in the church came and told me her husband wouldn't come to church, but he said that if we ever were to build a church he would give some money toward the building. I immediately made arrangements to meet with him and explained that I had found some choice property on 25th Street. When I told him exactly where it was he said, "You can't build a church there! That's swampland." I told him I realized the condition of the land, however, I really believed God wanted us to build there. I believed He would provide every need that we had.

I knew the first need we had was to fill in the land. But the man was adamant that it was totally ridiculous to consider building in that location. I learned that the people who lived next door to the land had a five-year-old son who had almost drowned in that swamp. So I could see where this older man thought that I was a young kid pastor who didn't know what he was doing!

I told him about a new family that was coming to the church – a man and his wife and five children – who let me know that whenever we were ready to build the church he would loan me his dump truck and skip loader to use anytime.

I told the older man that I believed God would give us the fill dirt we needed, even though it might be many hundreds of tons. I let him know that I had my eye on a place where they were taking out millions of tons of dirt to fill in Lake Michigan shoreline and expand the steel mills in Gary. My plan was to purchase the land, then go talk to the company, believing God would give us the fill dirt we needed. The man then reluctantly agreed to give me some money and told me to return the next day to take him to the bank. I was expecting more, but thanked the Lord for the $300 he gave me. I went immediately to the woman who owned the land and she agreed to take $300 down on a contract sale.

As soon as I signed the contract, I drove to the place where they were taking out the fill dirt. I found the man in charge of the operation, introduced myself and explained to him that we were sent by God to this area to establish a church. I told him we had just bought some land, explained to him where it was and admitted that it was swampland. I said, "We need a lot of fill dirt and we have no money, for my wife and I are living by faith."

"Sometimes we get $15 to $25 a week," I said, "and sometimes we get nothing. But I've been praying, and I believe the Lord told me to come and ask you to give us the fill dirt for our new church property."

Remember, I was only 22 years old. The man just looked at me.

Then I said, "Before you say anything, I want you to know I believe in prayer. And I will pray that God blesses you and blesses this business, and that He will keep your trucks and equipment from breaking down and He will keep them running smoothly."

I went on to tell him about the family that had just come into our church. I told him about the truck and the skip loader they had agreed to loan us for the building of the new church.

Praise God! He agreed to give us the fill dirt that we needed, free of charge! Needless to say I went from that place rejoicing, thanking God and praising Him for all the marvelous ways He was working on our behalf.

The next day I began hauling the fill dirt into the swampland where we were going to build a new church. It was only four or five miles away so I could haul many truckloads in a day. Then the next day I would take the skip loader and smooth out the dirt. Incidentally, I had never run a skip loader before, but the Lord guided my hand and helped me to complete this huge undertaking.

After the lot was filled in, I asked, "God, now what? We need money to put in a foundation. Where are we going to get the funds, Lord?"

Somewhere I came across a supply of little hammers with screwdrivers in the handle. Each time you would unscrew one, the screwdriver would become smaller. In 1948 this was a brand-new product on the market. We were able to buy them for 50 cents apiece and then sell them for a dollar. I went everywhere, telling people that we were going to build a church and these hammers would pay for the foundation. I had hammers in every pocket of my pants, in my coat pocket and in my inner pockets. I was really weighed down. I asked the people in the church to sell the hammers and explain what we were going to do, for we needed enough money to pay for the concrete that would go into the foundation.

I began digging the foundation, but I have to admit I didn't know what I was doing. I prayed and asked God to show me how to do it. For God, the Holy Spirit, is our teacher. Psalms 32:8 says, "I, the Lord will instruct you and teach you in the way you should go. I will guide you with my eye."

Digging the foundation became quite a challenge, because the fill that we used was sandy soil and I was digging down below the fill to the swamp and removing the top layer of dirt beneath the water. It was discouraging, because it seemed like every morning when I would arrive to work on the foundation, the sandy fill would have partially caved in where I had dug out the foundation on the previous day. As I was working, a man who was now coming to the church stopped by. And boy, did he bawl me out.

"Listen here," he snarled. "You're getting into way too big of a hurry in building this church. Trust me, I've learned a bit more in my 42 years than you have in your 22!"

I told him, "I'm sure you know more than I do. But God has sent me here to build this church building and establish a body of believers here."

"You're never going to get this done," he replied, shaking his head.

Slowly I reached out and handed him a shovel. I told him if he would get down and help me, we would get it done more quickly. He grumbled, and I turned around and continued to dig. Soon I heard a car door slam then a roar and off he went.

We did get the foundation in and again I asked, "Well Lord, what do we do now?" I already knew we were going to build a block building, but how were we going to pay for it? Where would we get the blocks and the mortar? Even though I had never laid blocks before, I was determined that the Lord would help me accomplish this task.

The idea came to me to have pictures of blocks printed up in booklet form – fifteen pages with four blocks per page. We would sell the blocks for 25 cents apiece or $15 per book. This would pay for the concrete blocks and for the mortar. I presented this to our little congregation and we went everywhere selling blocks.

Unfortunately, at the same time we were struggling to build the church, all the steel mills and oil refineries in the area were on strike. In those days in the Gary area, steel and oil were the main pillars of the economy. It became such a crisis that after many months President Truman had to invoke the Taft-Hartley law to force workers to return to work.

Things were very difficult, but God was faithful. Betty and I were still living by faith during all of this, giving our full time to the building of the body of Christ and the church building. We ate a lot of beans. Once someone brought us a case of eggs – 48 dozen. We ate fried eggs, boiled eggs, scrambled eggs and deviled eggs. Betty found many ways to prepare eggs and we thanked the Lord for those eggs.

During that first winter we were in Gary, we would go to bed early and cover up well to save money on heat. But we were happy because we knew we were in the center of God's will.

The pastor of a large nearby church came by one day to visit us in the chicken coop. When I opened the door he gasped and said, "Oh my, I didn't know you were suffering so!" The funniest thing was that we wouldn't have known we were suffering if he hadn't told us!

However, we were still excited and trusting God to do great things. We received enough money through the sale of the blocks in booklet form, so I bought the blocks and the mortar and the materials were delivered to the site. Even though I had never laid blocks before, I discovered it wasn't too difficult for me and I was coming along fine until I reached the level where I knew we needed to put in windows.

So I prayed, "Lord we're going to need some money to purchase the window frames." During the midweek service I explained this to the church and asked them to please pray. We could go no further until we had window frames. After the service, a man came to me and said, "I'll have window frames here for you tomorrow." I believe he had to borrow the funds on short term, but the frames were there the next day.

Up went the walls! One day, as I was laying blocks, one of church men came by and began to give me a tongue lashing saying, "You're spending too much money and in too big a hurry building this church!" He continued to rant, but I just kept laying blocks with tears streaming down my cheeks. Again I told God, "I know that you called me to do this and I will obey you." I didn't know you could have so many of Job's comforters in a small church but, like Nehemiah, I just kept building the wall and God continued helping and encouraging me. It really was so exciting to see the walls go up!

But once they were up, I found myself again asking the Lord, "Lord, I have no money and I can't go any farther. What should I do now?"

I didn't seem to get an immediate answer, so I thought I'd go to the bank. I dressed in my suit and tie and prayed, asking the Lord to give me favor. I presented our needs to the officer of the bank. I told him the story of the building of the church thus far and that we needed to borrow money to complete the building.

His first question was, "How many members do you have?"

I reluctantly admitted that we had five. "I don't mean the members of your board," he said. "What is the total membership of your church?" I repeated that we had just five members. He acted as though I had insulted him and let me know there was no chance of us borrowing money from them with only five members.

I went to several banks in the area and the reply was about the same. So I went before the Lord, asking, "Lord, what am I going to do? We need to get into this new building before winter comes."

Then I felt the Lord speaking to me, telling me to go to Henderlong Lumber Company. This was one of the largest lumber companies in our area, located about 30 miles away. I dressed up in my suit and went to the lumber company and asked if I could speak to the person who made the final decisions in the company. "Do you mean Mr. Henderlong?" asked the secretary.

"Does he make the final decisions here?" I asked.

"He is the owner," she replied.

"Then I'm sure he is the one I would like to speak with," I said.

She informed me I would have to make an appointment. But I confidently told her I really needed to speak to him that day. Unimpressed, she repeated that the company's policy required making an appointment.

I told her I had driven 30 miles to meet with him and I boldly asserted I felt God had sent me on a mission to talk to the head of this company. I stressed the urgency of the matter and let her know how much I would appreciate it if she would suspend the policy and let me see him for a few minutes.

Reluctantly, the secretary got on the intercom with Mr. Henderlong. Of course, his first response was to echo the policy requiring an appointment. The secretary proceed to tell him she had explained to me the appointment policy, but that I appeared very determined to see him. "He believes God has sent him here today to talk to you," she told him.

Mr. Henderlong relented and told the secretary to send me in. I strode right into his office, telling him how I appreciated this moment of his time. Starting at beginning, I shared with him how God had sent me to the Gary area to build a church. I went into detail, telling him about each step of the construction and concluding with our present dilemma. He stopped me a time or two and objected, "I really shouldn't be listening to you, because you're Protestant and I'm a Catholic. My priest wouldn't like this."

There was a great gulf in those days between the Protestants and Catholics in America. But despite his apprehensions, he let me continue, saying, "Somehow I am intrigued with what you're telling me."

I explained that we needed all the materials to finish the church. Then I went straight to the point. I asked him to furnish the materials on a payment plan.

He stopped me right there and said, "Do I understand that you laid the blocks for the church building … and you had never laid blocks before?"

"Yes sir," I answered.

Then he said that before he went any further he wanted to send his head mason to investigate the block walls and evaluate whether or not the building merited putting on a roof and supplying materials for completion.

He frankly reminded me that he would have more money in this project than we would. He told me to get back with him in a few days and he'd have a report from his head mason.

Of course I began to sweat. I was very nervous knowing that a professional was going to inspect my block-laying project.

We had no telephone, but I hurried back to town; drove to several of our congregants' homes and asked them to pray. I suggested they pray that God would make the mason blind to any flaws, mistakes or problems.

A few days later I drove back to the lumber company and walked into Mr. Henderlong's office. I asked if the head block mason had been over to inspect my work. He just kind of stared at me. Finally he said,

"I have high regards for the mason's opinion." Then he paused. Again he asked me, "Do I understand correctly that you laid the blocks?"

"Yes sir," I replied. "Is there a problem?"

"No," he said. "I'm just confused. I have every confidence in my head block mason and he says it is an excellent job. Yet you say you never laid blocks before."

Immediately, and with excitement I gushed, "That's great! When can we get the materials to finish the church?"

Mr. Henderlong slowed me down and explained that we needed to discuss several things. He was still very concerned about what his priest would say if he found out that he was helping to build a Protestant church. We discussed all the materials that we would need, starting with the roof. We would also need insulation, ceiling tiles, doors, hardware for the doors, all the electrical wiring and light fixtures...

"This project keeps growing, doesn't it?" interrupted Mr. Henderlong. Ignoring his remark I continued, "We will need a concrete floor and I truly want opalescent glass for the windows, because it resembles stained glass, which I know we can definitely not afford!"

He laughed and slowed me down again, telling me that Henderlong Lumber didn't deal in glass, cement, electrical wiring or light fixtures. He said, "You continue to intrigue me," he smiled. "I don't believe I've ever heard of one of our priests building a church ... or even repairing a rectory!"

He still wasn't quite sure why he was agreeing to engage in this project, but he had made a decision to go along with us! I assured him that we would pay him every month before I would receive a dime – even if it meant my having to acquire an outside job, I would see that he would be paid first of all. He responded saying, "We will provide all of the materials you need which we carry in stock. The other things you mentioned go ahead and purchase them as you need them and have the bills sent to me here at Henderlong Lumber Company."

Speaking very intently he said, "One requirement I will insist upon is that I have my architect draw up plans for the truss rafters for the roof."

Even though I didn't understand what truss rafters were, I told him several times we were extremely grateful and so appreciated his help.

A few days later we had all of the lumber materials along with the architectural plans for the truss rafters on our property. I looked at the plans for an hour or so and I was completely baffled. So I began to talk to the Lord. I said, "Lord I don't understand these plans. What does it mean to cut it on a specified pitch?"

I was totally confused and perplexed with everything on those plans. And as I continued to stand there and pray, I began to weep, saying, "Lord, I've got all this material here! What am I going to do with it? I understand nothing about these plans. I've come to the end of myself! I don't know anyone who I can get to help me, Lord! I have no money to hire anybody."

I began crying out to the Lord, "Send somebody to help me!" It seems like I was praying desperately for 10 or 15 minutes. I told God that if He could send someone who could make up a pattern and make a jig for me, then I could do it.

I continued to ask God to send someone to help me until suddenly I heard a voice to my left. I looked and there stood a man about three feet away. Out of his mouth came these words: "You need help, don't you? I've come to help you!"

I was completely astonished and thought to myself, *Where did this man come from, Lord?*

I looked quickly and saw no car, but here he was with a hammer in his hand, a nail apron on and a measuring tape on his belt!

Then he said, "I'll make a pattern truss for you and a jig and then you can make every one of these truss rafters, can't you?"

Again I was astounded to hear the same words coming out of his mouth that I had just asked of the Lord a few minutes before. I quickly agreed and he immediately went to work. He told me take the tape measure, explaining that he wanted to measure and see if the building was square. So we walked the wall and every few feet he measured. When we made our way around, he said it was perfect and he began to make the first rafter. While we were working I quizzed him as to where he lived.

"Oh, I live here and there," he answered cryptically.

I took notice as we were working that he never measured anything twice. Everything he did was always perfect the first time. I quickly came to realize that he did not sanction talking or questions while we worked. However, all the time he was there, my inquisitive mind was probing, Lord, where did he come from? Is this an angel? No, he couldn't be an angel, for he looks like a carpenter!

I felt so peaceful and blessed in his presence and was so confident and totally assured that he was doing everything right. I had perfect peace about it.

When he was finished, he asked if I had any other questions. Then he instructed me, "If you build every rafter just like I have shown you, I guarantee that they will fit perfectly on the walls when you hoist them up."

I believed him completely and thanked him once more. I noticed as he walked away that he went in the opposite direction from which he had come. I couldn't take my eyes off of him as he walked away, for I was thanking God for sending him. But I turned my head for a moment and when I looked back he had completely disappeared. I've never seen him since.

Later that evening I told my wife about this experience. We both rejoiced and praised God for this supernatural miracle, for as we pondered, prayed and thought about this, we both were convinced that God had sent His angel to help me. We kept this to ourselves for many years, as we believed that because we were young, no one would believe us. So many seemed to think we were already far out!

Next in God's master plan was the arriving of my 16-year-old brother, Lee. He thought he was coming to visit us for a week's vacation. However, he soon learned he came just in time to help me build all the rafters for the new church. We worked from sunup to sundown and sometimes into the night, with the lights of the car giving us light. He was a tremendous blessing. While he was there, we built all the rafters and they were completely ready to raise. God is a very present help in the time of need! Praise his name!

On Labor Day of 1952, we had rafter-raising day. With the help of other men from neighboring churches, we were able to raise all the rafters and get the roof on. The rafters fit perfectly on the walls, just as I was told that they would. It was so significant to witness a roof put on the church in one day! Praise God, there were two men who came every evening after work and they would work a few hours. One precious man, who was about 75 years old, would work during the day with me, mixing mortar and helping in every way that he could.

Over the next few weeks, the ceiling was insulated and tiled, the concrete floor was completed, the doors were hung, window glass was installed and the electrical lighting was installed. The ladies of the church came to help with painting and varnishing. On a Sunday in mid-October, we dedicated the new church to the Lord Jesus Christ. Only seven months after we began to build, we were moving from the single-car garage that would seat 40 or 50 people to our new building which would seat 200!

It was nearly full the first Sunday morning, with 185 in attendance. Needless to say, we were excited and praising God for the great miracles He had wrought. At 2 o'clock that Sunday afternoon there was standing room only for our formal dedication of the church to the Lord Jesus Christ! All of the visiting ministers and pastors were amazed at what God had done. Many said they never believed it could be done there, but God did it before we knew that it couldn't be done. All things are possible to them that believe! In fact, they used to call it the miracle church of the state of Indiana. This was the beginning of the miracles and the supernatural walk with God in the ministry for Betty and me.

CHAPTER FOUR

※

A Laodicea Church

Our church in Gary grew quickly. So quickly that only three months later it was necessary to construct another building, larger than the one we had just built. Naturally, we couldn't see any possible way to make this happen. But again, through a series of miracles, our awesome God brought it to pass in the summer of 1953. Many mountains were moved and many giants were slain. For God brought the victory; all the glory belongs to him.

It will soon be 60 years since the church was established there and two buildings erected. A second story has been added to the educational wing and other cosmetic improvements have been made since. No one can dispute it being one of the finest buildings in the whole area. We have been invited to minister there on several occasions, the last time being a little over a year ago. It blesses our hearts to see the church still progressing.

The two men who helped in building the church in the evenings both went into the ministry. One even pastored the church he help build! He then pastored several churches and just recently retired after pastoring a church in Highland, Indiana, for over 30 years. The other went to his reward in heaven a few years ago. In fact, there are six or eight that we know of who have gone from that church into the full-time ministry.

As Galatians 6:9 says, "Be not weary in well doing, for in due time you will reap the reward." I share these things to encourage you to believe in God for the impossible, always remembering that nothing is impossible with God.

By the way, after living in the chicken coop for a year, the Lord moved us into a real house. And a few months later, He supplied a better house across the street from the church, where we lived until we tendered our resignation.

From the church in Gary, the Lord called us to Harrodsburg, Indiana, a very small town in the southern part of the state. This was quite a change for us. But though it was a small town, it was an older, established church. There were times when there were more people attending a church service than there were in the population of the city.

These precious people loved the Lord and they also loved and embraced Betty and me, along with our first daughter, Sandra, who was six months old. They showered us with groceries: chicken, eggs, beef, potatoes and much more. They invited us to their homes for delicious meals. I had more time for study in preparing messages than I had previously. God blessed our ministry there and we stayed for about 20 months.

From there the Lord called us to Indianapolis, the capitol city of Indiana. This was a relatively new church, which had been in existence for six or seven years. There had been three pastors before us and they had just built their first new permanent building. We were there only a few weeks and immediately the church began to grow. I had the young married people's Sunday school class and within a couple of months we had totally outgrown our room. The downstairs basement auditorium, which would seat probably 60 or 70 people, was not being used. Our attendance was so large that for two consecutive Sundays we were forced to move into that auditorium. A good problem to have, I thought.

One evening, as my wife and I were out making calls, we went by the church and noticed all the basement lights were on. So I decided

I'd stop and see what was going on. When I got inside, I saw all of my board members were there. I asked if I'd called a board meeting and forgotten about it. They said no, but they might as well tell me now, that they had decided during this board meeting, called without me, that my class would be staying in the room designated for that class when I came here.

I addressed one of the board members, who was in the class, saying, "You know that class has grown and it is impossible for us all to even stand in that room!"

The board answered, "It makes no difference. We have decided that your class will stay in that room."

The spirit and attitude of this group was obviously being exposed. I said no more, but went back to the car. Immediately my wife asked, "Honey what's the matter?" She could tell that my mood had changed drastically. So I told her about the entire ordeal.

"There's no reason to go on with any more visitation," I decided. "I am just going home to write out my resignation and will turn it in on Sunday. It's impossible to do anything here. I'll have to turn over half my class away on Sunday and tell them there is no room. That, I am not willing to do!"

But when we got home, instead of making out my resignation, I began to pray. I continued all night. As I was waiting on the Lord, He told me not to resign, for He had sent me there. He gave me several scriptures and then told me exactly what to do on Sunday morning. I was still a very young man, only 26 years of age, but I knew the Lord's voice. He instructed me concerning the next Sunday morning, telling me that when it was time for the classes to go to their rooms, I was to go to the room in which the board had ordered me to remain.

He further instructed me, "You will find there will be more people who come to your class than ever before. So tell them: 'Obviously, we are not able to get into our regular classroom, so we will go into the basement auditorium.' "

The Lord instructed me to encourage them to give thanks for the blessing of the Lord and for those who were being saved. Then I was to tell them that our class would assemble in this basement auditorium from now on! By faith I was to make this declaration: "Very soon we will have to move this class to the upstairs auditorium, because of the blessing of the Lord and the growth that will happen in this church."

That morning, a couple of my board members were in the class. And if looks could kill, I would have been dead twice over. In fear and trembling I did what the Lord told me to do, confident that He was going to take care of everything. For I had learned early on that to obey is the best way! There was no doubt in my mind that this opposition was in no way from God. A spirit was manifesting that was against the blessing of the Lord! It was pride, arrogance, a spirit of control and **'ego'** (which, in this case, clearly meant "edging God out"). Though they had said they wanted to see the church grow, obviously they were afraid they were going to lose control.

This is a problem in many churches today. That's why in the book of Revelations, we see Jesus standing at the church door knocking. But in so many churches today, he can't get in! When He speaks of the Laodicea church, he's talking to the church that is controlled by man! I don't know this for sure, but I believe that very afternoon the board met to plan their strategy and decide how they were going to deal with my actions.

I had no doubt God was in charge of this whole situation, and it was confirmed to me when someone brought to my attention that one of the main leaders had a heart attack that Sunday afternoon. The next morning I rushed to the hospital to pray for him.

I never heard another word about our class meeting in the basement auditorium. God intervened as I had obeyed Him. His was a plan far above man's and the Lord had let me know that this was to become a large church. Within another six or eight months we had to move my class to the upstairs auditorium and rename it the "Pastor's Class." This class grew from a dozen people to 154!

During this time of growth and blessing, the original group of about 60 traditionalists continued to oppose every move we made. When new people participated during the church services, often the original ones would put their hands over their ears, shake their heads and react negatively.

During one board meeting, I presented over 30 people who wanted to become members of the church and who had applied for membership. The deacon board replied by saying, "We will not consider anyone for membership." This was the spirit that was manifesting, but God continued to overrule and was still blessing. Greater is He that sent us and is in us than he that is in the world!

At our first annual business meeting, a man stood up and said, "I would like to make a motion that we elect a new deacon board!" I had never said anything to anyone about my relationship with the board. I was shocked, but in my heart I asked, "Wow God, what's going on?" Almost immediately I noticed the deacon who had been giving me most of the trouble was shaking and trembling. Then he jumped out in the aisle and said, "I second the motion!"

When I acknowledged that we had a second to the motion and began to explain to folks how to mark their ballots, the deacon stood up and said he was withdrawing his second to the motion. As chairman of the meeting, I indicated that he couldn't withdraw a second to a motion, as per parliamentary procedure, unless the motion had been altered or changed in some way.

He said, "I don't care. I withdraw it anyway."

Believe this pastor when I tell you I knew it was necessary to study Parliamentary Law and Roberts Rules of Order very diligently. It quickly came to my mind that the Chairman could allow a second to a motion to be withdrawn if there was no objection by the body to the withdrawal.

So I explained this procedure and told them the Chair recommended that we allow him to withdraw his second, since he was one of the deacons.

Not surprisingly, we obtained another second to the motion and that is how God gave us a new deacon board in one year. I had nothing to do with it! God did it, so in the next year we were able to take in new members.

But this group continued to oppose everything that was said and done. Just before I would get up to preach they would verbally attack me with every negative thing they could find to say! Yet each time God would bless me and help me amazingly. God gave me grace so I could love them and shake their hands and continue to bless them for that next year. (Note: This was before hugging became common in the church!) It was quite obvious they were waiting for the next annual business meeting when they could vote on me again. They knew I needed a two-thirds majority vote. So they were doing everything they could to discourage and dissuade everyone before that meeting.

During that year I became the Presbyter of the Indianapolis section. This was most unusual due to my young age, so I felt the Lord wanted me to conduct the business meeting. Despite the opposition's efforts, during this meeting I received exactly two-thirds of the vote from the membership. One of the former deacons — the one who had been the Sunday school superintendent — yelled, "That's a draw!"

So I calmly clarified from the bylaws. "No," I said. "That's exactly a two-thirds majority vote, as required. The Chair declares an election!" The very first Sunday when I had arrived as a new pastor, this man had been in my face. From the beginning, he said, "I want you to know I run the Sunday School and you keep your hands off. It's not your affair."

Clearly, God had changed things and He determined to fulfill His plan, even though it was very difficult. I kept my eyes on Him and moved forward. About 60 of them never came back to the church. But even though they weren't there the next Sunday, we had more in attendance than we had the Sunday before.

God is faithful. If we'll obey him, he will bring his plans to completion. We stayed a total of seven years and the Lord used us in building and establishing a solid foundation. It was no longer under man's rule — now the Lord of the church was in the house!

This church in Indianapolis grew to be very large, complete with a television ministry that helped save thousands. They have a prayer tower with 24 hours of prayer support. They have numerous local ministries in the city as well as numerous foreign missionaries. The glory of the Lord is still in that house and praise be unto our great God! Scripture teaches us that we should not grow weary in well doing. For if we faint not, we will reap the reward. To God be all the praise and the glory forever!

We really wanted to stay in Indianapolis, as we knew God had great plans for that church and we so wanted to be part of it. But our ways and our thoughts are not His ways and His thoughts and neither are our plans always His plans.

So God called us to Saginaw, Michigan. Wherever God sent us, we always expected great things, even though we didn't know what the future would bring. The church we were called to had just built a new church building in a beautiful area. Again, the Lord let me know that He planned for this church to become a large church and have a great influence in the city and in the state of Michigan. To God be all the Glory!

I believe God has a plan for every person, every church and every ministry. But there must be total obedience to reach the full potential of God's plan and His purposes. This church had been in existence for about 50 years at the time we arrived. Five of the members had attended Bible college in Minneapolis at the same time I was there. Most of them graduated, and they were quite aware that I didn't really finish the first year.

But we were excited that God was sending us to the city of Saginaw to pastor what seemed to be a tremendous church. We arrived on a Thursday and, as I recall, there was a prescheduled board meeting for Friday evening. As all seven of the board members were seated, the head board member, who I understood had been in the church for about 40 years, leaned forward out of his chair and said, "I want to make one thing clear to you. Preachers come and go. I stay!"

So immediately I knew what my assignment here would be. Obviously it was another church ruled by man – a Laodicea church, neither hot nor cold, but lukewarm. I didn't say a word in response to him, but just smiled. I remembered that God had already let me know this was to be a large church, influential after his own heart. But He had to get in. Here again, he was standing at the church door knocking!

Revelations 3:16 says, "So, then, because thou art lukewarm and neither cold nor hot, I will spew thee out of my mouth." If we're not careful, we can become lukewarm, cold and indifferent toward the things of God! May the Lord help us to remain faithful and on fire for him. If we're on fire for the Lord, all of the fiery darts of the enemy will seem as nothing.

The challenge was immediately staring this young pastor in the face, for I further learned this church had not seen anyone saved at her altars for over five years. They never talked or prayed about anyone receiving the Holy Spirit or being healed. Certainly God was not really to blame that nothing was happening in their services.

It didn't take long to discover that the church was going through a lot of backbiting and fault finding. Dissension prevailed. The Lord let me know that He had sent me there to set the church in order and welcome the Holy Spirit and the Lord Jesus Christ to be the head of this body.

I soon found out this was the giant I had to face. But like David, I was confident that God was going with me. Evidently I had faced the lion and the bear before. Now I was to take care of my Goliath!

It was perfectly clear to me that these church members were skillful, smart and had been quite successful in their man-rule for a long time. This Jezebel spirit had to be removed, overcome, defeated and cast out, so God's plan could come to pass.

Immediately, God began to bless. The crowds increased and we began using the balcony for the first time in their history! People began to be saved and filled with the Spirit. The Lord began to move in marvelous ways: healings and deliverances became normal. One Sunday morning, a mother of one of the deacons got so happy, she came dancing down the aisle and shouting. Betty and I were shocked and saddened by the deacon's reaction. Instead of rejoicing with her, he hung his head in shame.

It didn't take long for opposition to arise in the church. For the devil couldn't stand what God was doing in that place, which he had bound and controlled for many years. A group led by the head board member wrote a petition against me and went to my superiors in the denomination.

When I met with these Godly men, their conclusion was that God had sent me there so the principalities and powers there could be broken down! My superiors were behind me one hundred percent. For over 20 years, they had tried to see a change in that church. They knew full well that it had been under man-rule for many, many years. They explained that this head board member had charge of all of the building finances and no one could ever see his financial records.

In addition, no one had been able to see the financial records of the general treasurer who was another controlling deacon.

There was great stress and pressure for some time. But I knew God was at work and He kept letting me know I had been sent there to break this seemingly impossible stronghold. He is the Spirit of truth and Jesus, the head of the church, wants to take control of His church. God continued working, moving by His Spirit, performing great signs, wonders and blessing in the services.

With His blessing behind us, it didn't take long before the opposing faction, led by this deacon and building fund treasurer, left to open another church. Despite their absence, the next Sunday we had more in attendance than the week before and God continued to bless as He was cleaning the house. Since so many members of this church were related, the division resulted in families split up – some leaving and others staying. Because of this, the Lord let me know that a root of the man-rule still remained in power. I could stay and He would bless me or His plan could be more expeditiously accomplished another way.

So about a year later, I went to the board and said, "I will resign, if all of you resign your positions. For we need to let our superiors appoint a pastor here and establish new leadership in this body." They agreed, so I went to my superiors and told them our plan. They were reluctant, because they said they didn't have a good church to offer me. But I persisted in persuading them.

"I know this is God's will," I said. "I'm ready to do what Jesus said, "Deny yourself and take up my cross and follow me." I knew God had told me this would be best for the church in the future, so I announced my resignation.

Betty and I sold everything we owned except for a few personal items, which would fit into a two-wheeled trailer. Two weeks later, I preached my farewell message. And, with the trailer hooked to the car, and with eight-year-old Sandi and her five-year-old sister, Cyndi, we headed out for California. We did not know what God had before us. But, again by faith, we were moving out in obedience to His plan.

A few years ago, we were able to go back to that Saginaw church and see what God had done. Our hearts rejoiced, for that church has become a large, influential body in the city of Saginaw and in the state of Michigan. It is a great missionary church and they have built a large new building in a strategic part of town. It was obvious that the Lord Jesus Christ, the head of the church, was in the house! Praise be to God, the Lord is able to perform that which he has promised.

CHAPTER FIVE

✂

God's Journey

All the way to California we drove only 30 to 35 miles per hour because the two-wheeled trailer would begin to sway dangerously if we went any faster. But the Lord helped us to control it and we arrived safely in the San Diego area. It was the day after Thanksgiving, 1963. My parents lived in National City, a little over 10 miles from downtown San Diego. We stayed with them for a few weeks while we were trying to find somewhere to live.

We didn't have much money and needed to find some way to sustain ourselves right away. Betty found a way to arrange imitation flowers and sell them at a gathering of ladies who came to a party. Obviously this didn't bring in much income. We had about $3,000 from the sale of our house in Indianapolis and from selling our furniture in Saginaw, so I purchasing a self-operated coin laundry to provide some income. It was open 24 hours a day. I would go early every morning to clean up and to make any repairs on the washers and dryers. I also had to service the coin-changing machines and was on call 24 hours a day in case there was any problem. One of the most common problems occurred when the water valves would stick on the washers and they would overflow, running all over the floor. Many times as I arrived, water was coming out the front door of the building.

The Lord began to open the doors immediately for ministry in various churches. I found myself preaching at least once or twice a week somewhere. Betty and I were in prayer most every day; asking the Lord to reveal his real purpose for us being in San Diego, for He always sent us where He wanted us to go. We knew He had some plan that we knew nothing about for this time.

We knew well that the Scriptures taught us, "Our ways are not His ways and our thoughts are not His thoughts, for as high as the heavens are above the earth, so His ways and thoughts are above ours!" Isaiah 55:8

"For I know the thoughts and the plans that I have for you, says the Lord; thoughts and plans for welfare and peace and not for evil; to give you hope in your final outcome." Jeremiah 29:11

One Sunday morning we were not ministering anywhere, so we decided to attend a certain church for the morning service. We arrived a few minutes late and left immediately after closing prayer. The next day, we receive a call from the pastor who asked, "You're a minister, aren't you?"

I answered yes and he said, "I knew it when you walked in the door of the church. I'm going to be gone for a couple of Sundays. And when you walked in, the Lord told me that you are the one to take care of the church and preach the two Sundays I'm going to be away."

He asked if I would do it for him and I said yes, but I added, "You don't know us. Are you sure about this?" He had no doubt about it. So we ministered there the next two Sundays and God did bless in a wonderful way.

We expected the pastor would return to his pulpit the next Sunday. But instead he called and asked us to minister again. And we were glad to glorify the Lord and see his people blessed once more. Even more surprising, when the pastor returned a few days later, he resigned and immediately the church asked me to become pastor.

So in March 1964, we became pastors of the church in the San Diego area. We had no doubt that God did this all supernaturally by himself. Many pastor friends tried to discourage us from coming to California as they warned us there were so many ministers sitting around waiting for churches. It was a graveyard for preachers!

As it happened, we had about six and a half wonderful, peaceful years with just the average, normal challenges of pastoring a church. We saw the attendance more than quadruple. Many gave their lives to Christ! We saw many healed, delivered from bondage and many filled with the Spirit. Overall, we enjoyed the blessing of the Lord as we pastored this church. This was clearly one of the easier assignments that the Lord had given to us.

Betty enjoyed leading and developing the choir. She and our daughters formed a trio and sang often in the church. My wife has always been involved in many areas of the church and if there was a position that needed to be filled and no one else would step forward to fill a vacant spot, she could always fill the need with her many God-given talents.

Eventually we began sensing in our spirits that our work at that church was coming to an end. We began to anticipate what God had in store for us next. Our commitment was still to seek first the kingdom of God and his righteousness. His will and purposes had always been and ever will be our heartbeat.

In late summer of 1969, the Lord led us to a church in Bakersfield, California. This was quite a change from the climate of San Diego. Bakersfield was in the San Joaquin Valley in central California and was surrounded by the desert. In the summer it was very hot – sometimes 110 degrees or more. We have always set our minds to be happy, wherever the Lord sends us. So the hot weather didn't bother us. The bottom line was, "Whatever the Lord wanted us to do, that's what we desired to do!"

The Lord provided a beautiful, brand-new home for us to purchase. This was our third new home, and many times we would think back to the days when we started in the ministry and lived in the chicken coop for a year. Over and over we would praise the Lord for his goodness! We were excited about our new pastorate and we were expecting God to do great things.

Within a few weeks the power God began to move in the services and the church attendance began to grow. Revival broke out with people being saved and filled with the Holy Spirit. There were many testimonies of healings and miracles.

One Saturday, in the middle of the night, a family called me to pray for their small child who had an extremely high fever. After prayer, the family left for the hospital emergency room. When they arrived, the child's temperature was totally normal and they could find absolutely nothing wrong. On the way to the hospital, the Lord healed what was most likely a case of contracted spinal meningitis. The next morning, the family was in worship service with their child, giving praise for the miracle that God had wrought.

The Lord did many wonderful things in the two years or so that we were there. And once again, He began to let me know that he was going to move us. I didn't know where we were going, but I was confident He was at work with the divine setup and had everything under control. A church in Redlands, California, was without a pastor and I was invited to fill the pulpit and minister on a particular Sunday morning and night service. They had two or three different ministers they were considering for pastor and these men were going to be preaching the following two or three Sundays.

The Holy Spirit moved in a powerful way in both the morning and evening services that Sunday when my family and I were there. It seemed the windows of heaven were open and pouring out refreshment. That night, the leaders requested that I be voted on as a pastor of this church. I was interested because a few years before this, I felt the Lord let me know that someday I would pastor this church. So I agreed to let the vote go forward.

When we left that evening to return to Bakersfield, I was the pastor of Redlands church. Needless to say, the other ministers who were vying to become pastor of the church the next three Sundays were very upset. It was extremely unusual how I became pastor. It just seemed like God opened the door and pushed me through it.

We returned to Bakersfield and I resigned from the church, effective in 30 days. We put our house on the market and advertised it ourselves with a sign in front of the house and an ad in the paper. It was a beautiful home. I had landscaped the large backyard and built a waterfall and a fountain. There were a couple of families who were very interested in purchasing it. But the Lord spoke to me and said He wanted the next pastor to have that house. He instructed me to take it off the market, take down the sign and remove the ad from the paper. I did, with no an idea who the next pastor would be and whether he would be able to, or even want to purchase the home. But God said so and I obeyed.

Within about a week the church selected the new pastor. When I found out he was elected, I called him at the motel and asked if we could meet. He agreed and we chatted at the motel for a little while. Then I invited him to come to our house for lunch. As we took him on a tour of our house and grounds he fell in love with everything. I asked him where he planned to live. He said he didn't know, but would probably try to rent or lease an apartment. He was in his forties and had a family. But, as he put it, "I don't have any money! I don't have two nickels to rub together. I may have to sell my car to move here."

My heart sank, but I told him the church would take care of the moving problem. I kept thinking about it though, until finally I asked, "How would you like to have this house?"

He laughed, thinking I was joking. But I told him I was serious. He sighed, "There is no possible way I could ever buy this property."

I took a deep breath and told him I knew this was going to sound strange but that God had told me the next pastor of the church was to have this house. In a flash it came to me how it could be possible. And

I told him, "Let's go talk to the president of my bank and see how much he will loan you on this house."

As we talked to the president of the bank, I impressed upon him that there had to be a way to make this happen, because the Lord told me the next pastor of the church was to have the house. I told the banker if he would make a loan to the new pastor, I would take a second loan and would pay all the closing costs, the title report and all expenses.

He said he just couldn't do that because the new pastor would have no money in the property. Urgently I explained that something had to be worked out because the Lord told me this pastor is to have this house!

Finally the banker said, "Well if you are this adamant about it, I'll go along with you, but this is highly unusual." So our house became the new pastor's house.

At that time, the new pastor's wife was in the hospital in Atlanta undergoing a hysterectomy. About two months later my wife and I met the pastor and his wife at a special meeting in Bakersfield. They told us how, when she first walked in the door of the house, she fell to the floor weeping and sobbing. She could not believe what the Lord had done for them! They lived in that house for about 20 years, until their retirement.

From that day forward, they continued to prosper greatly. God blessed them and He blessed us, as we were obedient to the Lord and we found a fine home in Redlands. Praise God. If we bless others, God will bless us!

In Redlands we prayed and asked God for His vision for the church, for the city and for us. A few years before our arrival, they had built a beautiful new church building. Immediately, we began to envision the church filled twice on Sunday morning. Betty and I said, "Let's just stay here for the next 25 or 30 years." We believed God wanted to build a large church here. And since we had moved around a lot as we followed the Lord in ministry, we thought perhaps He would let us stay here.

Over the next few years, the Lord did bless us and there were periods of time when we were tremendously excited about the future of the church. One week there were over 30 people who received the baptism of the Holy Spirit, speaking with other tongues.

We went to the church every morning, Monday through Friday, and for the first 30 or 40 minutes, we devoted ourselves to the Lord. We sought Him for His blessing in the church. We had always wanted to pattern each of the churches we pastored after the first church in the book of Acts. We would earnestly pray for signs, wonders and miracles that would lift up the wonderful name of Jesus our Lord and Savior.

In our fourth year there, as Betty and I knelt in prayer at the church every morning, I began to have visions of ministry overseas in missionary evangelism. It was a little confusing at first. However, over a period of months, the Lord continued to speak to my heart. At first I thought this couldn't be of God, for we had planned to stay here in Redlands for 25 or 30 years. But God continued to speak and the visions continued. I began to realize the obvious; our plans for the future were not His plans for our future!

CHAPTER SIX

❧

World Pentecostal Conference

In 1973, we attended the World Pentecostal Conference in Seoul, Korea. At that time the Lord opened doors for us to minister in Hong Kong and Japan. When we arrived in Korea, the Lord brought me together with a young man named gi-Chang Na, who was a pastor and just starting a church. We began talking as we were riding on the bus and he invited me to preach in his church on Sunday. I accepted and he came to our hotel to take us to the Sunday morning service.

When we drove up we were amazed because we had to walk across an open sewer in order to enter the building. In our country, pigpens were superior to this humble place of worship. gi-Chang Na had started the church in this place a year prior. When I ministered that morning I had to tip my head down low, otherwise, it would have touched the ceiling. The floor of the hut was the wet ground and the few people in attendance were sitting on the ground, for there were no chairs. Someone was kind enough to give Betty a cushion so her clothes wouldn't get wet. But God gave us a wonderful service and people were so blessed.

Almost immediately the Lord began to speak to my heart about helping the pastor build a new church. I didn't know how this would work, but I believed that God would bring about His plan. After the service, we went into the tiny room the pastor used for an office and talked about the work there. I asked him where he lived and he said, "Right here, in this little room."

"Where do you sleep?" I asked.

He pointed to one of the three chairs in the entire building, which were all in this small room. "You sleep in this chair? How do you do that?" I asked.

"I don't have much time to sleep," he replied. "So it doesn't make much difference where I sleep."

He told us about his busy schedule. He stayed up late calling and ministering to his people and studying for school classes.

He said, "In the morning at 4, I get up and go to prayer, because it is our custom in Korea to have early-morning prayer." After that, he told us he was going to school and learning to speak English and German.

Our hearts were stirred as we saw this devoted pastor and his work for the Kingdom of God. The calling in our hearts to help them build a church was getting louder and louder. This was the beginning of great changes in our direction in ministry. God was not just putting it in our hearts to help this church. He was calling us to gather the money so those people could worship in a new church building.

When we arrived home in Redlands, we sent them $1,000 almost immediately. We sent it to gi-Chang Na's superior, Pastor Yonggi Cho, to ensure there would be accountability for this young man. Pastor Cho wrote us a letter thanking us. Apparently this offering saved the land they were going to buy for the church property, since the landowner had another buyer interested in the property. Praise God, the provision arrived just in time!

This was the beginning of miracles for them and we continued sending many thousands of dollars. Over time, they were able to complete a beautiful new place of worship – all due to our faithful giving. We continued to receive letters from these people, filled with so much gratitude and so many reports of the great ways the Lord was blessing the work there. They were determined that we should come for the dedication of the building, but it just wasn't possible at that time. Still, it wasn't too many years later that we were able to minister again in that church.

In retrospect, we can see how God's plan was coming forth for our lives, bringing about drastic changes, even though I didn't understand completely at the time. More and more, the burden for missions was expanding in our hearts as our Father God was fitting us into His divine destiny!

CHAPTER SEVEN

1975: A Very Important Year

It was in 1975 that our lives began to change drastically. The Lord began to give me visions and I saw us flying to different countries, ministering. In my visions, I saw many people saved and many people miraculously healed.

These visions didn't line up with the plans I had, but God was speaking to me and telling me that He was going to bring us into a different ministry. My visions continued. I saw us flying to different places where people of different colors and nationalities were praising God with their hands upraised. God continued to fill my heart with these visions.

For a long time, I didn't say anything to my wife. I just pondered this in my spirit. Eventually though, I had to speak with her. I had to tell her how I felt God was calling us and was going to bring us into a traveling ministry. I didn't know how He was going to put all of this together, but I told her about the visions and how God was speaking to me.

To be honest, I found myself actually resisting this call. I knew my wife wasn't anxious to go, so I began to back off. But the more I backed off, the more it seemed that this thing in my heart would explode. God kept speaking to me, calling me to resign, to walk by faith and to trust Him. He was going to take us around the world in ministry.

One day, while we were at the church in prayer, the Lord lifted me up in the Spirit. He took me up through the roof of the building, high above. He said, "This is the way I look at the world. I want you to see it as I see it. When you minister in your local church, you preach to love one another and bless one another. But that is just the local church. I am going to send you to many countries and I am going to use you to bring this message from my heart to the people's hearts. I am going to use you powerfully as you trust in me."

The Lord let me know that He was going to send me forth as He did in Jeremiah 1:7. "I will send you where I want you to go and I will put my word in your mouth."

The Lord let me know that He didn't want me to be dependent on anyone but Him. He said, "I want you to resign the church and walk by faith. I never want you to ask anyone for an offering or solicit funds or ask for a meeting. I'll send you where I want you to go."

When I told my wife about all of this she was very concerned. She thought I was going through a mid-life crisis! But she sighed, smiled and agreed that, if we were going to resign and be in traveling ministry, she could contact many of our pastor friends, send letters and get meetings. She had been blessed with a wonderful gift for public relations.

When I grimaced and told her we couldn't ask for meetings or money, she just didn't understand. Truth be told, I didn't understand how God would bring this about either. But as an act of faith, I was to announce my resignation to be effective on the date He had given me, two months in the future.

I told the folks that I didn't know exactly what the Lord was going to do or how He was going to do it. But I relayed our burden and our commitment to do the will of God.

The time came when I was to preach my farewell message. My board came to me and asked, "Pastor has anything developed? Do you know any more than you did before?"

"I really don't know anything more," I replied. "The Lord hasn't said anything."

"We don't want to contradict you," they explained hesitantly. "But we just feel like you may have missed the will of God on this. And we want you to know that we believe we should all just carry on and forget about the resignation sermon tonight. Let's go forward and believe in God for great things!"

I thanked them. "Well, I appreciate your gesture," I said. "But I know that I must obey God. There is no other choice. I know it will be better for you and better for me."

I went ahead and preached the farewell message, even though I didn't know anything concerning the future. I simply knew that God was guiding me with His eye and that He was going to bring us into His plan and His purpose.

Chapter Eight

Selling the House

Many things happened over the next two months. God was working and speaking, but doors for evangelism weren't opening. We put our house on the market and placed a sign in front and an advertisement in the paper. Together, Betty and I agreed that the Lord would be our real estate agent. We were confident He would help us sell the house for we had peace even though it was listed higher than any house in the area. We certainly believed God would enable us to receive a good price, as He knew we would have many needs. He also knew we had no immediate hopes for a paycheck in the future!

While driving home from a meeting one evening I said, "Lord, we've had the house up for sale for over a month and haven't received even one phone call. What is going on? If we are in your will, doing what you say we are to do, you have to help us!"

As I was praying and driving, the Lord spoke to me and said, "The house is priced too low."

Startled, I responded, "What do you mean?"

"You named me your real estate agent!" said the Lord. "I want more money out of the house."

Immediately, I thought, "This is ridiculous. How could this be, God? How can I list the house at a higher price?"

I shared this with my wife and she was startled. She said, "It seems to me we need to lower the price!"

I had to agree. That would have been my thought as well.

But I replied, "God says the house should be priced several thousand dollars higher." When I told her the sale price, she gasped.

I changed the price in the paper, first thing in the morning. I admit we were both wondering, could this really be God? But this was only the beginning of the many miracles that God would perform for and through us this in this supernatural walk that He was now initiating.

We had learned much during our very first pastorate. God had directed us in ways that seemed far out to others. But now it seemed it was getting even more preposterous.

The next morning, as I was in prayer in my little office at the house, I was talking to the Lord about this situation when the doorbell rang. My wife answered and there was a real estate agent saying, "I have a client interested. Would you let me sell your house?"

My wife explained we were selling the home "by owner," and continued to say "My husband is very adamant about this decision."

The realtor insisted she must speak to me, so I told her, "This sale is in the hands of the Lord."

Again, she replied, "But I have a client who would buy this house."

I told her that we would not sign a contract because the Lord Jesus Christ was our real estate agent. She looked at me as though I was from another world, and I continued. "We must have a certain amount," and I gave her the figure the Lord gave me. She gasped and said there was no house in this area that would sell for that amount.

"If you can bring us a buyer who brings us this amount – net price – you may sell the house," I responded. The real estate agent left, shaking her head and saying she would contact us a little later.

About an hour later, she called and said her client wanted to see the house. The real estate agent brought a woman by, but as they walked through the house it seemed they didn't examine anything closely. The woman was only in the house four or five minutes. We decided that surely she wasn't interested.

Within an hour though, the agent called back and said her client's husband wanted to see the house. The husband and the agent came and again walked through very quickly. Betty and I decided that he didn't seem earnestly persuaded either.

To our astonishment, the agent called and said she had an offer. She relayed, "They will give you the exact amount that you want with the contingency that their house, which is already in escrow, closes and that the California Veteran's association will approval their loan. However, I have to warn you that qualifying with CalVet is very difficult. And with the price so inflated, I seriously doubt that the appraisal will be enough for loan approval."

I said, "Well if it is God's will, He will work it out." We reiterated to the agent that, if she expected to make money on the sale of the house, she would have to make a side agreement with her clients. We must have the total price we had listed, and no less.

To our amazement, the loan went through. In fact, it whizzed through. And we had to do nothing. The real estate agent took care of all the paperwork and brought us a check for the exact amount we had asked for. God was beginning to work marvelous miracles and we were excited. In the meantime, we were still fasting, praying and calling out, "Lord, you just have to show us what to do!"

CHAPTER NINE

※

Full Gospel Business Men

One Saturday night I was praying and the Lord told me to go to a Full Gospel Business Men's Fellowship International meeting. Now I had never sanctioned or supported FGBMFI because I felt that they were just businessmen trying to be preachers. If they were going to have church, I felt they should not be in cafeterias, ballrooms and hotels, but in a church building. To the contrary, the Lord was telling me he wanted me to go a FGBMFI meeting.

At the time, I knew no one who was even associated with this group. In the past, I had received their Voice magazine, but I would just throw it in the trash. I hadn't received one for many years. So I told the Lord that if he wanted me to go to a meeting, someone would have to invite me.

Shortly afterward, our daughters came home for a weekend visit from Costa Mesa College in Southern California. Betty and I planned to take them back to college on Sunday afternoon, then attend evening church service somewhere in the area. We chose a church that seated about 1,500 people and, since, we arrived quite early, we sat down about three or four pews from the front. The church began to fill up, but a few vacant seats remained next to us. As I looked around I saw that the main auditorium nearly full, and so was the balcony. This was, after all, an Easter production. As time for the service neared, a couple finally came to take the seats next to us. Before he even sat down, the man greeted me and introduced himself. "I am the president of the Santa Ana Full Gospel Business Men's Fellowship International," he said, and he proceeded to invite me to attend the meeting on Wednesday.

I was astounded. In fact, I began to weep. I asked, "God, what is going on? You really do want me to go to an FGBMFI meeting!"

So, on the next Wednesday, I attended the noon luncheon. I was introduced to the group and asked to share a bit of my testimony in the meeting. I tried to explain to them what God was doing in my life. "I am an unemployed pastor," I said. "God is just cleaning my clock and working me over."

They all applauded.

That was weird, I thought. They should have empathy for me. Why are they applauding? But it seemed that what I was sharing was proving to be a blessing, so I continued to tell my story. And when I returned home, God continued to pour out His blessing, even though I still didn't know what I was doing.

After we sold our home in Redlands, we moved to the city of Orange. Daily, we would search our hearts, pray, fast and cry out to God. Yet it seemed like the heavens were as brass. God wasn't saying anything and we didn't know what to do.

We continued praying, "Lord we obeyed you and did what you told us to do. Why aren't doors opening up? Lord help us."

We had no regular income from ministry. In fact, from April to the end of the year, our total income from ministry was $767. We were certainly crying out to God, yet it seemed there were no answers. Betty and I had every version of the Bible open, covering our entire family room floor. If the Lord spoke, we wanted to research anything He would say from the Word. We would fast and pray for two or three days, then eat for a couple of days, then fast and pray again. All the while we were searching and obeying the Bible as it exhorts us to ask, seek and knock. We were crying out for God's direction.

Of course the enemy was using the inactivity to grow seeds of doubt within us and make us wonder if we had missed God. But we just kept pressing toward the mark and prize of the high calling of Christ Jesus, and we continued to believe. He gave us the vision and now He would give the provision.

We claimed the verse in Proverbs 3:5-6, "Trust in the Lord with all your heart and lean not on your own understanding. In all your ways acknowledge Him and He will direct your paths."

God was teaching, cleansing, purging and pruning our hearts – causing us to put full trust and confidence in Him. For a number of years we had pastored established churches with a good salary, expense accounts and all the perks that come with a solid ministry. Now we could not look to man.

The Lord seemed to make it plain to us that we were not to pastor a church. However, from the time of my resignation in late February until late summer of 1975, I kept getting offers from outstanding churches in Porterville, Newhall, Fontana, Anaheim and Fresno in California and even from Scottsdale, Arizona. We cannot say we were not tempted to consider these offers.

One day a call came from one of these churches. I tried to explain what God was doing in our lives. I suppose I was not convincing in my answer, because they called a few days later, telling me some of the wonderful amenities they had to offer and describing their own youth ranch. It was very tempting, so I said, "I don't have anywhere to preach this Sunday and I could come and preach for you, but I can't let you think I will be your pastor, for God is leading me otherwise."

Betty heard this conversation and she just walked away shaking her head. When I concluded the phone conversation, Betty sat down on the sofa with her elbows on her knees and held her face in her hands. "Honey, are you alright?" I asked.

Her face was white as she said, "I just hope you know what you are doing!"

The truth is I didn't. So I just walked away saying, "Oh God, you are in control!"

I must admit, I would have normally been very interested in pastoring these churches. But I was compelled to turn them down for I had to press toward the vision He had placed before us. It was as if He was taking us through the school of absolute trust! Amazingly, for the next year, I continued to get offers urging me to consider pastoring churches in Lakewood and Bakersfield, California, and also from a large church in Houston, Texas.

After I attended the first FGBMFI meeting, we were invited to several different meetings and I shared briefly at each of them. At one meeting, someone mentioned that the FGBMFI were having a national convention in Anaheim, which was very near where we were living. They invited us to attend and offered to buy all our meals. We accepted and were thrilled to attend the convention over the next few days.

One morning at breakfast, there were at least 5,000 people in attendance and God was at work in a wonderful way. Founder Demos Shakarian and other leaders were sharing their burden and decision to build a new headquarters for the FGBMFI. He described the land they wanted to purchase in "a strategic location off a major freeway in the area."

He explained that it would require millions of dollars for the land and construction. But when he finished stating his vision and burden, a woman abruptly stepped up on the platform and spoke against the FGBMFI plan. I saw in the spirit a heavy cloud that came over the entire breakfast.

As she continued, God began speaking to me. He said, "When she concludes, I want you to go up there and I will give you a word that will break the back of the enemy and his plan to stop what the FGBMFI are trying to accomplish."

I said, "Lord they won't let me up there on the platform. They don't know me." By this time, Demos was speaking again and the Lord kept dealing with me. Finally I was compelled to jump up from my seat. It was like the Lord was kicking me in the seat of the pants! I headed toward the stage from my seat in the far back. I went to the back of the platform and started to go up the steps. A man stopped me, saying, "No, you can't go up there."

I replied that I felt like I had a word from the Lord that would be a blessing.

The man replied, "Demos has given instruction that no one else is allowed on the platform."

In my heart I grumbled, "God, I told you they wouldn't let me on the platform."

I kept trying to persuade the man behind the stage until Demos turned around quickly and said, "Let that man come onto the platform."

To my amazement, Demos just handed me the microphone. I began to tell the audience that I was an unemployed pastor and I didn't know how God was going to accomplish what I felt he had told me to do. I shared the story of how the Lord told me to attend the FGBMFI meeting even though I was not a fan of the organization. I spoke to them honestly, telling them how I originally believed this ministry could not be of God because the meetings were held in hotels, cafeterias and restaurants and not in churches.

Then I said, "But the Lord showed me that he has raised this organization up and has ordained you for ministry in these last days. God has convicted me and I want to confess and repent to Demos."

Demos and I embraced and wept. Then I continued, "The Lord has sent me to this platform to give $5,000 from the sale of my house toward the purchase of this land and for the building of the new headquarters. As I mentioned, I am unemployed and I don't know exactly what is going to happen in my future or how the Lord is going to bring forth the visions He has given me. But He has told me to give this offering out of the sale of my home."

Almost immediately, something broke in the Spirit and the whole atmosphere changed. Men and women left their seats from all over that vast auditorium and it seemed they ran up and threw money on the platform. Thousands of dollars came in and for several months people continued to give. The enemy who wanted to stop the building of their new headquarters was broken and totally defeated.

Later, I was told that letters would arrive, saying, "Remember the convention when that unemployed pastor spoke and gave $5,000 from the sale of his house? The Lord spoke to me to do the same thing, and so enclosed is my offering."

To God be the glory for the great things he has done! Demos gave me a lifetime membership in the Fellowship. He said I was only the second pastor to be given that honor. The Full Gospel Business Men's Fellowship International built and occupied a beautiful building for many years until Demos went to heaven. The building was then sold to Trinity Broadcasting Network (TBN) and is their main headquarters in Orange County.

In 1975, the Lord let me know there would be times in our ministry that we would be on television. The door first opened on TBN, in a studio in California, and we were able to share our testimony of the miraculous ways God was working in our lives. I also appeared on TBN for one week reading the Word of God. We traveled to Arizona to be on TBN in Phoenix and were on the World Harvest program in Indianapolis, Indiana. We were guests on Christian Television Network in San Diego and also had a program for the church where I was an associate pastor. We were on television in the Farmington, New Mexico, area and helped launch the television ministry in Keokuk, Iowa.

I also was guest and ministered in Salt Lake City, Utah; Tucson, Arizona; El Paso, Texas, and Atlantic City, New Jersey. God opened all the doors, allowing me to lift up and glorify His name, touching multitudes of lives as He fulfilled all He had put in my heart and promised to do.

CHAPTER TEN

❧

God's Word to Us

Gradually the Lord began to open doors through the Fellowship. He had a plan that was far beyond my imagination! He began to use us in a new way, far beyond our understanding and still we were not sure what He had in store for us. We were just willing to obey without complete understanding.

After that convention, I was invited to be a speaker for several FGBMFI meetings in California, and we were invited to appear on a television program on Trinity Broadcasting Network. On the show, Paul and Joyce Toberty interviewed us. It was a great blessing to share what God was doing in our lives. The musical guest for the night was Vicky Jamison, from Tulsa. Because she was on a different part of the set, Vicky did not hear our testimonies while we were on the show. After singing, she joined us on our set.

Vicky was greatly used in the prophetic and as soon as we were introduced, she began to prophesy. We never forgot this word from the Lord. "God's hand and anointing are upon you in a new and great way," Vicky told us. "You are being tested; shucked like corn. Many times you have cried out to God, hiding yourself behind locked doors and sobbing, 'Oh God, where are you? Have you forgotten me?'

"No, He has not forgotten. For you will preach in many churches of many denominations and minister to the masses. You will especially minister to the one, to the individual, on a one-to-one basis. You will be anointed mightily and when you lay hands on people they will instantly receive the Holy Spirit and many will be instantly healed. You have said, like Caleb, 'Give me this mountain!' You will take mountain after mountain for the Glory of God!"

This bolstered our spirits greatly, especially Betty, for she had not received the visions as I had. She was asking God for confirmation from those who had no knowledge of our past or present.

During this same timeframe, we were invited to attend a meeting in Santa Barbara. It was a long drive from where we lived, but we felt very strongly that we should attend. We were totally unfamiliar with the speaker, Dick Mills. However, his message reached us powerfully. He called many people forward after his message and quoted scriptures, which spoke directly to their lives, and they were blessed.

We were so surprised when he pointed to us and asked us to come to the front. He said, "I usually give scriptures from the Word of God to individuals, but the Lord has told me to prophesy over this couple. God's eyes are upon you. He has watched you and you have proven yourselves to be strong in His eyes. Yeah, He has known all your frustrations and the great turmoil of your souls. But through all this, the hand of the Lord is now empowering you to go forth in His name."

Dick continued, "The Lord says 'I am closing the doors behind you and you are going through a time of transition and waiting upon me. This is not a time of shame or confusion but is to strengthen your faith.'

"You are dying to the opinions of your friends, your family, your peers and your denomination and all of your own old ideas are being torn down. God is doing a new thing in your lives. He is giving you a new joy and bringing you a new freedom! He is now empowering you with a new strength! There shall be no looking back. He is shutting the old doors behind you and new doors will soon open before you. He will say to you, 'This is the way. Walk ye in it!'

"He will give you great favor in the eyes of the world. You will be used as a liberator; bringing release and restoration to many. You will be greatly used in the last day Revival that will be worldwide. You will find an open path into the historic denominations. You will be a restorer and refiner of the breech. You will build up the tabernacle of David and bring new life to the old places.

"The Lord says, 'Walk with me one day, one moment at a time and I will lead you beside still waters.' "

Needless to say, this was a most significant day in our lives. We could not have possibly remembered all these words, for all during the prophetic word the Holy Spirit so powerfully touched us. But Dick's wife took complete notes and gave them to us, We were visible shaking and not even able to stand. What a tremendous, magnificent confirmation, straight from the heart of our God whom we served!

CHAPTER ELEVEN

✁

Ministering From Coast to Coast

I n September 1975, I was invited to go on a ministry airlift to Italy and Sicily with the Full Gospel Business Men's Fellowship International. I felt God was opening the door and I told Betty I thought she should come along. But I would only pay her fare to Philadelphia, where we were to meet the group. I felt this was an opportunity for her to exercise her faith and to see how the Lord would come through for her.

We were assigned to minister with a group going to Palermo, Sicily. It is impossible to share all the memorable miracles the Lord performed by His power while we were in Italy. Many were saved and filled with the Holy Spirit, healed and delivered. We met wonderful people during this airlift who would become very dear to us. Some of them became extremely influential in our future ministry.

From April through December 1975, we ministered at churches in Anaheim Hills, La Habra, Bell Gardens, Anaheim, Simi Valley, Santa Monica and North Ridge, California. I also spoke for FGBMFI functions in Santa Ana, Covina, San Bernardino County, Pasadena, Palm Springs and Banning, California. Many lives were touched by

God's power, confirming what the Lord had spoken to me and through the prophetic words given to us.

In January 1976, Betty and I held a revival in a Bell Gardens church and it proved to be a week of miracles. Later in the month we were planning on going to Philadelphia, where the International Director of the FGBMFI had invited me. I was sent a ticket to fly to the area but, again, I believed that Betty should go with me. So she had begun believing God for her ticket.

The pastor of the Bell Gardens church was a very precious man of God whom we had known for many years. He was so excited about our new ministry because he had seen how people were being powerfully ministered to by the gifts of the Spirit. He was a rare friend, because most of my peers were convinced that I had gone way out in left field! He knew that Betty needed a ticket for the ministry in Philadelphia, so he started what he called a "kitty." This invitation to minister became a prototype which God used to show us we did not have to ask for meetings or for money.

The revival was glorious and most of God's family who were present received individual ministry from His precious Holy Spirit and His gifts. And the "kitty" for Betty's ticket amounted to a total of $289 – more than enough.

In Philadelphia, we were met at the airport and taken to a motel in nearby Trevose. It was extremely cold and the ground was covered with snow. The meeting was held in the motor lodge and it was exceptionally powerful. Many of the people attending had never seen God's gifts in operation. At least 12 came forward for salvation and many were slain in the Spirit for the first time.

The next day, our host and his wife came and took us to their beautiful home along the Delaware River. They took us for a long drive through beautiful small towns and we ate lunch at a charming restaurant. We ended our trip with a drive through the Princeton University Campus. It was a fabulous day!

That evening there was a Bible study in the same room of the motor lodge and about 100 people were there. There were just so many hungry people, and

God met all their needs. The next day we were treated with such care. We were picked up by a pastor and his wife who entertained us and we spoke at their church in Morrisville, Pennsylvania. We also attended a regional rally in Washington, D.C., and then went to Atlantic City, New Jersey, where we shared on a local television station and spoke at a breakfast of the FGBMFI. Finally, we took a bus to the Liberty Bell and its museum – remember, this was 1976, and the entire year was a bicentennial celebration! The Lord accomplished so many things while we were on that trip and we were grateful for having been provided our tickets and wonderful fellowship.

On our way home, it was arranged for us to stop in Arizona to attend the annual FGBMFI Convention in Phoenix. When I arrived, Demos Shakarian informed me that I would be the main speaker at the next morning's breakfast meeting! God anointed me powerfully; the Holy Spirit touched many with His gifts and many miracles of healing were evident. After this service, and throughout the convention, I received invitations to minister in Jackson, Mississippi, for their State Convention in June, in Illinois, in Phoenix and in Grand Junction, Colorado. The doors continued to open! We were invited to preach in a large church there in Phoenix, and the pastor purchased both our tickets to return home to Orange County.

During 1976 we spoke at churches in La Habra, Baldwin Park, Los Angles, Vacaville, Downey, Desert Hot Springs, Milpetas, Shafter and Simi Valley in California. In addition, I ministered at FGBMFI meetings in Westchester, Concord, San Juan Capistrano, Desert Hot Springs, Livermore, Marin County, Sacramento, Fremont, Antioch, San Francisco, Salinas, Vacaville, Red Bluff, Santa Rosa, Riverside and Hemet, California. In May, I was the speaker at the Northern California Men's Advance in Santa Rosa.

In early April we flew to Grand Junction, Colorado, to speak at FGBMFI meetings there and in Glenwood Springs. We also ministered at two churches in the area.

Also in April, I flew to Phoenix to be a guest on PTL with the Crouches on their new Phoenix TV station. We stayed to speak at a

Phoenix FGBMFI meeting on Saturday morning and at the Prescott Chapter on Saturday evening. I ministered in a church there on Sunday morning and in a home meeting in the afternoon.

That April I was also invited be one of the speakers on an airlift with FGBMFI to Sweden and Brussels. We left on Saturday, April 16 and flew first to Chicago. There, we spoke at an evening banquet for the local chapter. The next morning, I taught a Sunday school class in a large church; then spoke to a Philippino Catholic Mass in the afternoon where they asked me to close the service and many miracles happened.

We flew on to Sweden where I ministered in Stockholm at Engelbrect Lutheran, Slussen Pentecostal and Sion Pentecostal Churches. Betty and I were assigned to travel by train to Western Sweden for ministry at the following churches and cities: Sattchan, Filipstad, two services in the Karlstad Baptist, and two services in the Karlstad Filadelphia Pentecost Church.

Some of the cities were as many as 60 to 100 miles apart. We traveled very far to the Gullspang Missionary Baptist Church, and then to our last service in Kristinehamn at the Filadelphia Pentecost Church, where people drove in from many other churches.

It was a tremendous service and marvelous miracles happened while we were there. There was such a powerful anointing as I called out sicknesses. The Lord was doing such outstanding wonders. People had been falling in the Spirit in all the meetings. (This was a first in Western Sweden!) But this service was so powerful. When I ministered to the pastor, head elders and other elders, they were all on the floor. Then I touched the head of my interpreter, a lovely young woman named Gunella, and she fell to the floor. Of course, as my interpreter, she was vital to the service and I had to get her up so I could continue the service! Miracles kept happening until 11:30 p.m., when Gunella had to leave for her home.

This was a fantastic move of God. We found the Swedish people to be so warm, friendly and very hungry to receive the present move of God. When we left on May 5, to return to Stockholm, many came to see us off. They were in tears, knowing we might never again see each other until we all arrived in heaven. We left the next day for a convention in Brussels and it was there I met a pastor from Greece who invited us to Macedonia.

On June 3, we flew to Jackson, Mississippi, where I was the speaker at their three-day FGBMFI State Convention. God's power was evident in all the meetings. The International Director and his wife, precious people, then took us to their home city, Laurel, where we ministered for seven services. The Lord did unbelievable wonders in Mississippi and we were destined to return.

We flew from Jackson to Detroit, Michigan, where an International Director had set up meetings in three churches and two FGBMFI banquets in different areas. God showed up in a precious way and continued to bless, save, heal, fill with His Holy Spirit, deliver and do signs and wonders.

In early July, we went to Miami for an FGBMFI convention. God miraculously took care of our hotel and meals while we were there. After the convention we rented a car and were privileged to travel all around Florida for about a week. Then we flew to Bloomington, Illinois, where meetings were scheduled in seven churches and groups (two were in a barn) and two Chapter Banquets. We also spoke in Champlain, Leroy Park, Morton, Normal and Mackinaw. I was honored also to speak at a Chanute Air Force Base Chapel service. The mighty power of the Holy Spirit did His work in every service.

CHAPTER TWELVE

❦

A Burden for Korea

In June of that hectic 1976, the Lord began telling me that we were going to South Korea in ministry. I waited for awhile, trusting that He would speak more details, because I wanted to share this with Betty. But I heard no more. So finally I just said, "Honey, the Lord has told me we are going to South Korea to minister."

When Betty asked how, when and where, I replied, "He didn't say."

Betty turned and walked away, disappointed. I was just as disappointed that the Lord had not said more. But I still believed that He would bring to pass His plan and purpose for us in South Korea, in His timing.

Shortly after this word, the Lord called us to attend an upcoming meeting where there would be 500 people present. I reluctantly agreed. Betty and I arrived and took our seats about halfway toward the back. The meeting progressed and a visitor from Seoul, Korea, named Pastor So was introduced. He was asked to share and when he stood, up the Lord said to my spirit, "This is the man you will minister with in Korea."

I thought, How could this happen? He doesn't know me. I pondered this in my spirit (and didn't say anything to Betty). Pastor So spoke for just a few minutes and sat down.

When the service was over and we were exiting down the center aisle, I saw Pastor So, leaning against a pew near the rear of the church. I had to nearly run into him to get by and I thought about what the Lord had said earlier. As I walked closer to him he appeared to want to talk to me. We greeted one another and I told him I appreciated his sharing.

Pastor So said, "I don't know exactly why I am here. They scheduled me to preach in several churches next month, but they have everything mixed up. Still, I am sure the Lord must have some reason for me to be here."

All of a sudden it was as if a thousand-watt bulb turned on.

"Now I know why I am here," he exclaimed. "The Lord told me I would meet a man with a burden for my country who will come to my country and minister. He is telling me that I am to set up the meetings for as long as you want to be in Korea. I am to be your host and your interpreter. God is speaking this to me. Will you come?"

I was totally amazed at how God had brought this invitation to me and I told him I would come.

Pastor So continued, "I am the pastor of a very large church. We are in the same building that Pastor Cho used until he built his new building. Our church is growing very fast. I don't have time to do this, but the Lord is telling me you must come."

We set up a meeting in Korea for a few months later in the spring of 1977. My faith was not great and I figured the Lord needed the time to get the money together. I had no idea how He would accomplish this.

In the meantime, we continued traveling and ministering in churches and various chapters of the FGBMFI. During this time, we had several confirmations from the Lord that we were to move back to San Diego. God sent many friends to help us, including an old friend from Kokomo, Indiana. This friend was driving a large, empty moving van and just happened to be in the area when we were to move. What a blessing!

As the date approached for us to leave for Korea, I prayed to the Lord, saying, "You know we are to leave next Thursday and we only have $300 toward our Korea trip. We need $3,000 at the very minimum. Lord, if you don't do something quickly I don't know what we will do!"

The Lord spoke to me, not with an answer as to how we would get the money we needed, but instead he told me to give $100 to a certain ministry. I wasn't very excited about giving to this ministry, as it was one I didn't really care for. Still, the Lord had spoken and said to do it. I told Betty … though I knew she would not be thrilled. But since it was the Lord's instruction, she wrote the check and put it in the mail.

At the same time, the Lord also told me to go to an FGBMFI breakfast in Anaheim. The drive from San Diego to Orange County was about 100 miles, so we left early in the morning. It was only a few days until we were scheduled to board the plane to Korea.

Betty said, "Honey if the money doesn't come in for both of us, why don't you just go ahead and go." I told her I believed God would meet the need very soon, even though I wasn't sure how.

When we arrived at the breakfast, we greeted our precious friends who were in leadership. We told them we were leaving for Korea the next Thursday, but we didn't mention our need for money as we were still under the Lord's instructions not to ask.

During the meeting, one of the men in leadership suddenly spoke to those in attendance. "Howard and Betty are leaving Thursday for Korea," he told them. "The Lord has spoken to us that we should pay Betty's way and He has said we are to give her $1000."

I rejoiced – God was speaking and something was happening! Since they were passing the plate to pay for Betty's expenses, I began wondering if Betty might need to take over the ministry. They hadn't said anything about me!

I was puzzled. We had talked about me going by myself, but now this money was designated for Betty. The Leader of the meeting had made that plain and I knew I could not touch it for myself. It seemed strange, but we rejoiced and continued to believe that the Lord would somehow put this together so we could both go.

As we were driving home from the breakfast, the Lord spoke to me, saying we should attend a local Baptist church for tomorrow's morning service. We had never been there before, but at an earlier meeting we met a couple who asked us to visit this church.

They said, "We don't have any position or authority at our Baptist church, but the Lord is really speaking to us, saying that you should come and visit sometime."

We had them write down their names, along with the name and address of the church and we assured them that we would pray about it. They placed the paper with the information in my pocket while I continued to minister to other folks.

As I drove home, I asked Betty if she remembered that incident and I told her the paper with the information was at home on the dresser. The church was located in El Cajon, about 20 miles from our home.

The next morning, we arrived at the church during the last 15 minutes of the Sunday school hour. I asked an usher if he would seat us by the couple who had invited us to visit. The usher said they were not there yet but would probably come for the morning worship. Betty and I decided to sit near the back and asked the usher if he would mind bringing those people to us if they should arrive. They never came. But I handed the usher one of my cards and asked him if he would let these people know that we had come to their church.

At that moment, the pastor came by and the usher introduced us to him and handed him our card. After a few words of introduction, he told us how glad he was that we were there and he had to go start the service.

The pastor began the service with announcements, praise and worship. Then the pastor said, "Folks, something has happened to me that is unique in my 20 years of pastoring. A moment ago, I shook hands with a man I have never seen before. I just can't preach this morning, for I know this man has to preach. I don't understand it – I've never had anything like this happen before."

He told the congregation that he had asked his staff if they noticed the man in the back raising his hands during worship (a unique sight in a Baptist church) and if they sensed anything about him or got any vibes from him. Their answer was no.

"I have his card and I see that he sings, so he can come and do what he needs to do," the pastor continued. "Folks, I don't know what is going to happen, but I know that I have obeyed God."

So Betty and I went to the platform and I sang and she accompanied me on the piano. I shared how God had been leading us since 1975, and I told the congregation about some of the miraculous events and ways He was supernaturally using us.

I shared how the Lord had taken us to Sicily. I told them of the many wonderful things God had done there and that we were blessed and privileged to minister in Italy. I told them the story of a man we'd met in Palermo who had never been in the church before. God touched him and he was healed as a large tumor on the side of his stomach disappeared. The man had begun to excitedly jump around. He didn't understand what was going on but he knew the tumor was gone. He came back the next night with all his medical records and shared what the Lord had done. He told us he had just slept over eight hours without a shot of Novocain in his side and without pills to ease the pain. He didn't understand all this but he was jumping around like a kangaroo and we told him to give the Lord all the glory and honor and praise for this miracle of healing.

I continued telling the congregation at this Baptist church about preaching nearly a week in Palermo and then traveling to Bagheria to minister. I told them about the time when, after a Sunday service in Bagheria, some came to the altar to be saved. In my heart, I had asked the Lord what I should do next; should I pray for the sick? The Lord told me to speak deliverance to those who had demonic activity in their life and to ask those people to stand. I carefully explained through my interpreter, and was amazed that a couple dozen people stood.

Surely, I thought, this many do not need to be delivered from demonic activity. I felt certain something had been lost during the translation through the interpreter. So I explained it again very clearly and distinctly; thinking most of the people would sit down. Instead, several more people stood up.

I thought, God, I can't pray for this many people. We need to leave soon, for I am committed to other services. We have only a short amount of time!

Then Lord told me to pray for all of them at the same time. I wanted to be scriptural, so I told the Lord that I didn't remember Him casting out demons other than one at a time.

The Lord said to me, "Didn't I tell you that greater things you would do because of the Father? Pray the prayer, speak the word and I'll do the work."

The congregation at that Baptist church listened with rapt attention as I told them how we prayed through the interpreter and began to bind the enemy and command him to leave. We had continued this until, all of a sudden, all over the building in Bagheria, there was great noise. People were being thrown to the floor. To my right, a man started kicking over benches. He was slithering like a snake, but roaring like a lion. This was a great move of the Spirit of God and people were being set free by the power of God.

One woman got up and said, "I'm so glad I've been set free."

I told the Baptist church how they brought the man who was roaring and slithering to the altar area. I told the interpreter to ask him what the Lord was doing in his life. My interpreter was reluctant. He was as white as a ghost because of the strange things that were happening at that meeting. I went down, taking my interpreter, and approached the man who was on his knees with the two from our group who had brought him to the front.

I told the slithering man, "I want you to praise the Lord." When he opened his mouth he was still roaring like a lion and slithering like a snake.

I looked at him and spoke to the evil spirit with authority saying, "Leave him! I will not speak to you again. In the mighty, powerful name of Jesus; the blood is against you. Be free in Jesus' name."

After that prayer the man was able to raise his hands and praise the Lord and give Him honor and glory saying, "Gloria Jesu."

At that point, a woman had stood up and said, "That man is my husband and he came to the altar this morning to be saved. I am so glad he is released from demons."

The Lord did great things in that one Sunday morning service in Sicily, leaving us to marvel at the power of God. Many were set free; many were saved and many were healed. We left that place rejoicing for what the Lord had done.

What I didn't know then but learned later was that many people in the area were involved in witchcraft. That explained why there were so many who stood in need of deliverance. We had never been in a meeting like that one before and we've never seen one since. I wish we had it on tape or film.

By the time I finished sharing all this with the Baptist church, I was ready to turn the pulpit back to the pastor. But the Lord pointed out a couple sitting near the front. He wanted me to minister to them.

"Lord," I protested, "I am in a Baptist church!"

He said, "I know. Still, I want you to minister to them." So I pointed them out. And as I ministered to them they began to weep. God continued to bless in a special way as I ministered to others that day in the gifts of the Spirit. I pointed to a couple of women toward the rear of the church and asked them to stand. As I ministered, the power of God touched them and they fell out under the power of God. People were all looking and wondering what was going on in their Baptist church, but God was moving in a precious way.

Then I turned to the left and the Lord led me to a couple and He gave me a word for them. When I concluded, I said to the pastor, "I hope I have not created any kind of problems for you. It has been a joy to be here. I pray God will bless you."

The pastor got up and put his arm around my shoulder. I was glad for that gesture, because I had constantly been aware of a side door and wondered a few times if he would take me by the seat of my pants and usher me out.

Instead he said, "I don't know what has happened here this morning. I don't understand it all, but I know it was God and this church will never be the same again! God has done something very special, but don't ask me to explain it. I believe we will understand more as we continue to walk with the Lord."

Then he turned and said to me, "I know that you don't know this couple sitting right down here, but you told them their problem and you had the right answer. I always feel I have answers for everyone who comes to me. But you, without knowing them, told them the problem and gave them the right answer."

He then pointed to the left and said, "That couple over there; I know you don't know them, but that is my daughter and son-in-law. And what you said to them is true as well. I don't understand this. I have never seen this before, but we know that God has been in our midst today. You said you were going into ministry in Korea?"

I told him yes, and that we were leaving on Thursday.

He replied, "Well this ministry must take a lot of money."

I nodded and he asked, "How does God supply your needs?"

I began to stutter, because, of course, our need had not been fully supplied. And I knew that I wasn't supposed to ever say anything.

The pastor cupped his hands and smiled, "Do you just say, 'God, I need $10,000' and it just appears in your hands?"

"No, He uses people," I replied.

"Well God is going to use us today," he laughed. "I am going to receive an offering for your ministry."

To our surprise, the Baptist congregation gave us a large offering and informed us it was the largest single missions offering they had ever received. There were probably 400 to 500 people in the service that morning. God greatly blessed us through them! We were astounded and rejoiced in what the Lord had accomplished.

It was totally supernatural how I was asked to preach when we just went to visit. God set the pastor aside and put us in the pulpit before we realized what was happening. God is so great and awesome He can do anything if we will trust in him.

When we arrived home, we got a phone call from someone in Orange County. It was a friend whom I had known for some time. He said, "Oh, I am so glad I got a hold of you! God has been telling me to send you some money. I tried to reach you (we had no answering machine back then!) and I have to get the money to you. God is telling me to do it now. What is going on?"

I told him we were leaving for Korea and he confirmed immediately that the money must be for that trip. "How can we get together?" he asked.

I had to be up in that area on Tuesday to pick up the check at the FGBMFI office for Betty, so we made plans for me to stop by and see him as well. I drove up to his office and found a parking place three or four doors down from his office. As I got out of the car, a woman ran out of an office. "Wait a minute sir," she called, "I have got to get you some money."

I was astounded, but I took the money and thanked her. She immediately went back into the building, not even identifying herself. As I walked into my friend's office I told him about the woman and asked if he knew anyone in the office a few doors down. He thought about it for a moment, but couldn't remember anyone he knew there.

I could not keep from rejoicing when he gave me several hundred dollars. I thought, Wow Lord, I should have asked for more so we could have spending money! I left, believing God for the future.

And God did provide all the funds we needed by the time we left that Thursday. Praise God, He supplies all our needs according to his riches in glory by Christ Jesus. God will meet every need when we trust Him. (Sometimes it gets awfully close, but I thank God for he is never late!)

Chapter Thirteen

A Vision Fulfilled

We left for Korea, knowing that God was sending us on this missionary journey. And we arrived in Seoul expecting great things. We ministered there for a week in the Westgate Full Gospel Church with Pastor So, who had invited us to come to Korea and acted as our interpreter. Over the course of the week, there were some 75 people who accepted the Lord and there were many miracles of healing.

We also spoke in a Bible school there in the city. And on the second Sunday there we were privileged to speak in the church for which we had given all the building funds necessary to build the church back in 1974. They were so excited at our coming and planned an extensive service and dinner in our honor, held at a beautiful home. It was such a blessing and a great joy to see what had been achieved through our giving. They had built a beautiful church and were accomplishing great things for the kingdom. We were served a delicious meal and shared delightful fellowship with some of God's precious family. Our hearts leaped for joy that the building had been completed and that we had a big part in helping it happen.

Through another supernatural arrangement by the Holy Spirit, we journeyed to Daejon to minister in the church of Foursquare Gospel. The pastor, Mrs. Seen Ok AHN, had escaped North Korea some years earlier and had established the church and Dae-Sun High School, which now had 10,000 students. Betty and I ministered daily in school chapel services out in the field and also in other classes where we shared the love of Jesus and how God had great plans for their lives. For seven days and nights, we ministered in the church, staying in the church guest quarters. We heard the dedicated Christians praying night after night, all through the night.

During this time, Betty was amazed to recall a vision she had when she received the Baptism of the Holy Spirit at 12 years of age. In her vision, she had seen herself standing before thousands of young Asian people who were all dressed exactly the same. She shared this with her pastor's wife and her mother who confirmed the Lord was calling her to special service, but that she should hide this in her heart and let the Lord bring it to pass. Her mother added, "But for this to happen, you must marry the right man!"

Betty had never shared this with me, for she thought we were called to be pastors. But of course, God had changed our calling and the vision came to pass just exactly as she had seen it so many years before. It was an awesome time for her, confirming again God's perfect plan for her destiny.

The next week we traveled far south with Pastor So, our interpreter, to the city of NamWon, where we ministered for five nights. Most of the residents of this town had never seen Americans and were enamored with our skin, hair and clothing. (Unfortunately, we were not likewise enamored with their restaurants and food – enough said!) Many accepted the Lord and God's miracles and blessings were abundant there. We could tell you many supernatural stories in which God did many wonderful things. Be encouraged, for if God tells you to do something, just keep believing Him. Keep pressing toward the mark and keep the vision before you. The Lord will do what He says He will do, even if He takes you up to the last moments and it looks like He will not come through. Our experience has shown us time and again – **God will do what he says He will do!**

Chapter Fourteen

❧

On Fire for God

When we left Korea our hearts rejoiced and we were refreshed, knowing that God had ministered to the people in such a great way. We were impressed to see the hunger in the people's hearts all throughout Korea and it was refreshing for us to see in some services that people would run to the altar to give their hearts to the Lord Jesus Christ. It is no wonder that Korea has enjoyed a great, wonderful revival and the largest church in the world is located in Seoul, Korea. Many times in their immense hunger for God, they would spend 30 to 40 days in fasting and prayer for revival in Korea and in the entire world.

When we returned home from Korea we were blessed to find in the mail an invitation from the Baptist church where we ministered the Sunday before we left to go to Korea, asking us to be speakers at their missions convention in a few weeks. There were to be five missionary couples representing different countries and I was asked to be the main speaker. That was a great blessing. God continued to use us in that church and soon we were asked us to join the staff!

We prayed about it and felt the Lord wanted us to join them, with the condition that we would be free to continue to travel as the Lord was calling and leading us. They agreed and addressed me as the Charismatic Pastor. As we worshipped and progressed in the things of the Spirit together, the church bought a large bowling alley, which they remodeled and to which the congregation moved. The church continued to grow and we began a weekly service on Tuesday evenings, which we called Charismatic Life. We taught on the Baptism of the Holy Spirit, speaking in tongues and the Gifts of the Spirit. And we conducted a School of the Spirit.

After teaching at length on each of the spiritual gifts found in I Corinthians, Chapter 12, we would have the people exercise each gift. God blessed in a tremendous way and there were many baptized in the Holy Spirit, speaking in other tongues. At first, many of them would say, "I already have the Holy Spirit. I received Him when I was saved!"

"Yes that is true," I would reply. "But our Lord Jesus Christ wants to baptize you, drench you and submerge you in the Holy Spirit. When He does that, you will go forth in the power and the might of His glory and will be able to do miracles, signs and wonders, as you will have faith in the Lord." These Baptists were then so receptive! Over the next couple of years we saw hundreds there receive the Holy Spirit, and God blessed in wonderful ways.

The Lord had obviously prepared the people's hearts for our ministry, as they were so hungry for greater things from God and just expected Him to do **great** things!

As people continued to be filled with the Spirit and blessed, the church became "Bapticostal." The church was on fire for God and became a leading church in that area. It was so exciting to see what our Lord was doing amongst the people. More and more in the Charismatic Life services, people were receiving and operating in the Gifts of the Spirit. They were prophesying, speaking in tongues, giving messages and having words of knowledge.

It was an exciting time, but I would admonish those attending the Charismatic Life class to not practice these gifts in the main services. Wisdom told me to be discrete, for the time would come when God would cause the pastor to release these gifts in the main services in an orderly fashion.

Finally, that day arrived when the gifts were released and God was moving in marvelous ways. The pastor's wife had a ladies meeting on Tuesday mornings with nearly 200 attending. At times Betty would hear her remarking, "We aren't sure what Brother Skinner is doing to our Baptist church."

I got the feeling she was opposing the move of the Holy Spirit, because many of the women from her meeting were attending Charismatic Life services, which we held on Tuesday evenings. Several, in fact, were receiving the Holy Spirit. The pastor's wife was obviously upset, so we tried to use wisdom and obey exactly what the Lord was saying.

One morning I answered our door and it was the pastor's wife. I invited her in and asked how I could help her. She said that she had come, first of all, to apologize. She had been fighting against my teaching that the initial evidence in receiving the baptism of the Spirit was speaking in other tongues. Then she proceeded to tell us that God had been dealing with her and that she had come this morning, ready to receive the baptism.

I asked her if she understood that when I lead people to receive the baptism of the Holy Spirit, I ask them to repeat a prayer. She said she knew and was ready to receive. She repeated the prayer and when I laid hands on her, like an explosion, she came forth speaking and glorifying God in a new heavenly language. It was a great refreshing time in our living room and the pastor's wife left praising God.

My wife decided she would to go to the next women's meeting to see what happened. "I want you all to know that you have a changed pastor's wife," the pastor's wife said. "I have been fighting this baptism of the Holy Spirit and speaking with other tongues for awhile. But last week I went to Brother Skinner's home and received the baptism of the Holy Spirit. And now I speak with other tongues."

She then jumped up on a chair and began speaking with other tongues! She exclaimed, "Every one of you women is going to receive this glorious gift of the Holy Spirit, for it's real and it's wonderful."

The whole atmosphere of the church seemed to change from that time on. This "Bapticostal" church was growing more and more on fire for God and we saw great and marvelous things as the Lord moved freely in our midst. The pastor was not experienced in the operation of the spiritual gifts of the Holy Spirit, but he was open and anxious to see all of them. Many times, he would suddenly ask me to come and minister in the word of knowledge. I had to be prepared at all times.

One Sunday evening, a couple brought the worship leader to the service in a wheelchair. He was a big, strapping, muscular guy and I wondered what had happened to him. The Lord spoke to me and said I should tell him to get up out of the wheelchair and be healed. I didn't pay any attention at first because, at that time, there weren't many manifestations of healing or miracles happening in the main services. At that time, most Baptists didn't believe in divine healing.

I tried to ignore what the Lord was saying, but He only came back stronger, saying, "In my name, I want you to speak to him. Tell him to get up out of the wheelchair and walk!"

"Lord, he has no faith," I argued. "Look at his face."

I continued to talk to the Lord, finally telling Him, "If you really want this to happen, let the pastor make an opening for me to act on this." I simply needed more confirmation. Almost immediately, the pastor asked me, "Howard, is there something you can do here in about ten minutes?"

I nodded yes and the pastor said, "Whatever the Lord is telling you to do, get up and do it."

There was someone singing at the time and the pastor told me as soon as the music concluded, I could take the microphone. As I left the platform, the Lord gave me a few specific words to pray for a few people. I remember thinking that I should pray for a few easier cases first! God was gracious and healed a few precious people and I suddenly realized that I had taken up my 10 minutes. I was still very apprehensive and started to walk back toward the pastor with the microphone.

Suddenly I wheeled around, addressing the brother in the wheelchair. "In the name of Jesus, rise up and walk, for the Lord is healing you." Instead of being excited, like I thought he would be, his head went down. I was concerned, but at the same time I kept doing what the Lord had instructed me to do. I kept commanding the man to get up and walk.

"I told you he didn't have any faith!" I said to the Lord.

I suppose I repeated the same command to him at least seven or eight times. On the ninth time his head came up. By this point I was praying the rapture would happen or **something** of paramount significance that would remove me from this situation, because it wasn't going well at all.

But I kept hoping the Lord would perform an Acts, Chapter 3 moment, equal to the time Peter and John took the lame man by the hand and commanded him to walk and he went away walking and leaping and praising God.

Finally the man in the wheelchair looked at me. So I focused on his eyes and said, "The Lord Jesus heals you. By your faith, rise up out of that wheelchair and walk in Jesus' name!"

His face contorted with great anguish and distress as he took one leg and moved it from the footrest to the floor. I did not react to his apparent pain but again commanded, "In Jesus name, be healed and rise up and walk."

He rose up, though it was evident the great pain still remained. He began to take small steps across the wide platform. He walked back and forth five times, each time moving slightly faster and gaining strength. On the sixth time he took one foot like a bull and began to scrape it on the floor, then made a dash, running across the platform and back again. As excitement in the crowd was increasing, he descended the platform and walked briskly around the outside aisle of the sanctuary.

The pastor and his wife ran down after him and then about two-thirds of the congregation followed in a hilarious, old-fashioned, Jericho march. I was **so** relieved and grateful to the Holy Spirit for His powerful intervention! It was a glorious sight as they continued marching in circles.

I thought to myself, The Pentecostals would not believe what has happened in this Baptist church!

God's blessing was evident and we glorified Him for His healing miracles. After the service we learned that the man had pushed his own wheelchair back to the hospital and we were told the complete story surrounding this miracle:

God had spoken to a couple, directing them to get this man out of the hospital and bring him to evening service. He was in traction and great pain but they insisted they were taking him to the service. He and some of the staff were very resistant. He kept telling them he didn't want to go to church. They argued, insisting God had given them an order to take him to this service and no amount of agitation deterred them. They assured the nurses they would return him after the service.

The hospital staff was finally persuaded and they brought the man to church. But the look on his face showed a man who was present against his will. They reminded me of the friends in Mark 2:3-5 who cut a hole in the roof to lower the man sick with palsy in front of Jesus to be healed. Jesus commended their faith.

We were told there were some people in the service that evening who walked out during this event. They returned on Wednesday evening and said they just couldn't bear seeing that Brother Skinner demanding their worship leader to get up out of his wheelchair when he was in so much pain. So they just left.

The people they were talking with said, "You left too soon! Look, there he goes now, walking to the platform to lead worship!"

God certainly began to change hearts and do many miracles during this time. We give God all the glory. I agree with Jesus when He said, "Without me you can do nothing."

Paul said, "I can do all things through Christ who strengthens me." We just rejoice in the miracles and the way that God moved so supernaturally.

We are about to see a great movement of God in this world very soon. God is getting the Church prepared, so I feel constrained with everything that is in me to encourage you to open your heart to the Lord. Let Him move in your heart to bless you. He is going to use the body of Christ. There are not enough apostles, prophets, evangelists, pastors and teachers to get the job done. God's word teaches us He is unequivocally going to use the body of Christ now.

In I Corinthians, chapter 12, Paul teaches us that the body of Christ has nine spiritual gifts that are available to us. The gift of tongues, interpretation of tongues, prophecy, gifts of healing, discerning of spirits, word of knowledge, word of wisdom, faith and the working of miracles. All these gifts are being poured out in abundance. So study this chapter and begin to pray for God to use you.

I'm excited, because I see God actively preparing His body. Soon even you may be facing unavoidable situations that you don't understand. You may be in the fiery furnace, but I assure you that Jesus is in there with you. He is making you strong as He did Joseph. Oh how He wants us to be strong, full of faith and full of power, going forth praying for the sick and laying hands upon them.

The Bible says that those who believe shall lay hands on the sick and they shall recover. Remember all the gifts of the Spirit are for the whole body of Christ, not just for the apostles, prophets, evangelists, pastors and teachers. Seek the Lord as to how He desires to move in your life, for He wants to abundantly use your life. He has spiritual gifts that are within you already and you can do great signs and wonders, if you trust in Him. Hallelujah, the greatest is yet to come!

CHAPTER FIFTEEN

※

Memories of Other Unusual Miracles

On one occasion during ministry, I called a man up to the front of the service. He was a deep-sea fisherman – a rough-cut type out of San Diego. I could smell alcohol on him, but the Lord gave me a word for him. God ministered to him and touched his heart. The Lord led me to minister to him in healing. I did not know this man had no kneecap, as it had been surgically removed. When I prayed for him, he suddenly cried out and began hitting his knee. He said, "I have a kneecap!"

It was an exciting, glorious miracle that the Lord performed in that man's life. His wife had been praying for him for some time and now he was marvelously converted and he ardently followed after the Lord.

A month or two later, he and his crew were out fishing. Suddenly he began to catch fish in great numbers such as he had never seen before. There were so many that he quickly filled his boat and called one of his buddies on the radio. His friend came and filled his boat as well. Everyone gathered at the docks to see the new San Diego species of fish that had yet to be named. The fish were delicious and brought a tremendous price, so everyone agreed this was some kind of a miracle.

I suppose that when Peter and this brother meet in heaven they will really have some fish stories to tell!

While the Baptist church was remodeling the bowling alley, we worshipped in a tent. There were many healings that occurred during that time, so we often gave opportunities during services for testimonies from the healed. One Sunday, a small man in his mid-seventies came forward. He was weeping and I kept asking if he could tell us what the Lord had done for him. Still weeping, he said God had done so much, he didn't know where to start. He said he felt so good he didn't know what to say or the proper way to express himself. It was so exciting to see people touched.

I recall another occasion, praying for a man who had one leg much shorter than the other and wore a built-up shoe about four to five inches high. As I prayed, the short leg shot out. The man was totally healed and could not walk until he took off both shoes. Then, as he carried them around, he walked out of the service normally, thanking and praising the Lord for his miracle!

Another time I called out healings for someone with a thyroid condition. A woman responded after the service, telling me her thyroid had been removed and she was on replacement medication. She returned later to report to me that she had not taken her medication for many months, but when they checked her thyroid level, it was completely normal. God can do anything if we just trust in Him. I look back to many things He has done and I give God glory.

One woman who came for prayer had been stricken with polio when she was a child, leaving one leg noticeably affected. When she sat in a chair and extended both legs, one was inches shorter and slimmer in diameter. As I was praying for her, the Lord instantly lengthened her leg before our eyes and it also grew to the same size around as the other leg. We all were praising God and were amazed.

She went and told her Lutheran church and asked if I could come and minister in their church. The next Sunday, they were having a

Bible school graduation. I had never met the pastor, but I felt it was a miraculous, God-given appointment.

When they introduced me I began to lift up the name of the Lord Jesus Christ and share some recent miracles He had been doing. They all were acquainted with the woman who had been healed of the leg deformity and were already excited to see the power of God in action. As the Holy Spirit began to anoint me, I called to the front the people who wanted prayer. God moved and began to do miracles and people were slain in the Spirit.

I noticed a gentleman kneeling down by some of those who were under the power of the Holy Spirit. I was told it was the pastor, who was a bit upset and he was patting them on the cheek to help bring them around. He thought they had fainted. I told him not to worry that it was a work of the Lord. I was not invited to return, but praise be to the Lord they got a taste of the real power of God.

The Baptist church had a weekly television program that aired for a half hour and they asked me to host the program for a period of time. This was quite a change, because I was bringing forth a new format and those watching for the Baptist flavor were now seeing the power of God and the charismatic flow of the Holy Spirit. It brought new people into the church and was a glorious time as the Lord was moving so precious in the hearts and lives of the people.

I've been asked how God opens doors for me and puts the words He wants me to speak in my mouth. Revelations 3:8 says, "The Holy Spirit sets before me an open door."

God supernaturally sets up meetings, using key people as though they are my agents sent from God. Most of the time it requires us being at the right place at the right time. Betty and I have found that we must be very sensitive to the leading of the Holy Spirit. We had to attend the right churches and meetings, eat at the right restaurants and even travel on the proper buses.

For example, one time we thought we were boarding an English bus to go to the World Pentecostal Conference, but it was the German bus.

An Asian pastor who was riding the bus was learning to speak English and German. He was looking for an opportunity to practice with the Germans, but was delighted when he found an American pastor and could invite him to his church to speak on Sunday. That's how God arranged for us to meet Pastor gi-Chang Na so we could preach in his little church in Seoul, Korea, in 1973. This was the beginning of our life's ministry change.

Invitations for meetings in different countries began to manifest in 1976. We had been overseas on two airlifts with the Full Gospel Business Men's Fellowship International, however, now it seemed the invitations coming were not related and were indeed supernatural!

As I was standing in a hotel lobby in Brussels, just before returning to the United States after our Swedish ministry in 1976, the Lord began to tell me to speak to the man standing beside us. I had never seen this man before. The Lord said, "He is a minister and I want you to talk to him."

"Excuse me," I began, "are you a minister?"

The man looked a bit startled, but replied, "Yes."

I asked, "Are you an evangelist, pastor or teacher?"

He said he was a pastor and almost immediately, with great excitement and emphasis he said, "You're the man! You're the man! You're the man!"

He spoke so fast, he was almost breathless. He told us how he was desperately seeking the Lord to send someone to his country who operated in a double ministry. (He meant signs and wonders.) The Lord told him to come to this convention and he would meet the man. He said he had spoken to a well-known missionary evangelist from Tulsa and a leading pastor from Houston. They had both declined, so he was discouraged and decided to go home that morning. But the Lord spoke and told him he had not yet met the man. "I know that you're the man to come to Macedonia and help us," He exclaimed.

Out of curiosity, I asked when he wanted me to come. "Right now!" he said.

I told him it wasn't possible for me to come now. I had several meetings in the states coming up. But we exchanged information and I told him, in God's timing, I would come to Macedonia. It seemed I remembered hearing that call several thousand years ago, "Come to Macedonia and help us!"

In just a few weeks I met another man in Northern California who was the uncle of a missionary in Athens. We talked for a bit and soon I also had an invitation to the one of the leading Full Gospel churches in Athens. (Gradually I had learned not to question the unusual and amazing ways in which God sets up meetings!)

Another time, Betty and I were in the Los Angeles airport and I began to feel God's spirit coaxing me toward another area. My wife tagged along, probably wondering where I was going. I walked past a couple who were both reading magazines. God told me to talk to them, because they were both missionaries. I walked back and forth in front of them, hoping that they would stop reading and perhaps look up. Finally God said, "Just speak to them."

So I hesitantly asked, "Excuse me, are you missionaries?"

They both gave me puzzled looks, probably wondering where we had met before, since they didn't recognize me. We began talking about their work in Sri Lanka and, by the time the call came for boarding, the Lord had put us on the same plane.

We sat together in fellowship and, during the course of the conversation, the man told us, "Our meeting you today is very strange, but quite significant. My wife and I were planning our flight for tomorrow, but the Lord kept telling us to go today. We couldn't understand, because our speaking engagement is for Sunday, and going today meant sitting around a day early. But the Lord was insistent that we go today."

"We were distressed, thinking tomorrow's flight might meet with disaster, so we decided to follow His instructions and go on this flight. Now, God is telling to us to invite you to hold an open-air crusade in Sri Lanka. If you would be willing to come, we'll start making plans, so let's kept in touch." This is how God supernaturally set up the meeting in Sri Lanka.

During the same time period, I attended a convention in Palm Springs, where I met General Woo from Taipei, Taiwan. After I ministered, He invited me to come to his country to hold meetings and he assured me he would make all the arrangements.

I recall a time in Louisiana when I met a pastor and, while we were talking during lunch, he invited me to minister in his church. That following Sunday during the message, the Lord changed my message 180 degrees and I found myself taking powerful authority and addressing the demonic force that was coming against that church and their pastor. We literally drove the devil out of the church by the power of God and the Lord gave a tremendous release that morning.

Three months later, the church leaders reported that the completely impossible situation they faced had been miraculously turned around. The enemy's hold was broken and they were now going forth in victory by the power of God. The situation which the church and pastor faced had looked absolutely hopeless at the time we were there, but now this wonderful deliverance had enabled them to go forward. We have ministered in that church many times since this victory, and God continues to move in His mighty power.

Can you see how God has supernaturally set up assignments for us many times? For the Spirit of the Lord will do great works when we obey and totally trust in Him. It is exciting as we keep on learning to **walk supernaturally** with Him.

My desire is to see the **supernatural** come alive in the church today. I believe it is going to happen in a phenomenal way. Jesus is building His church and the gates of hell shall **not** prevail against it. Jesus is Lord and He is the head of the church.

Pastors, if you look to Him, He will bring you through whatever you are facing. The giant will come down and the mountain will be made small! The Lord will give you great and glorious spiritual power over all the powers of the enemy as you walk and depend upon Him.

It really amazes me to see how God continues to build His church. When I consider the material He has to use (you and me), it is amazing that He has been able to bring the church to where it is today. Praise God! He has the ability to do it and nothing will stop what He plans to do. Let us put our full trust in Him. I have learned that when God gives a vision, if it truly is a God-given vision, there is provision.

Chapter Sixteen

Ministering Around the World

In 1978, Betty and I prepared to travel around the world in ministry. God had set up all the meetings and brought to pass what I thought was His perfect plan and itinerary. It wasn't until we arrived at the airport and boarded the plane that Betty asked, "Honey, what are we going to do? We don't have enough money to take care of our personal needs."

"Oh, we have enough to get to India," I responded calmly.

"Then what?" she persisted, undeterred.

"This is God's problem," I reflected. "He set up all the meetings around the world. So somehow, He is going to take care of us."

I did have money in savings that I could have used, but the Lord told me that we were to depend on Him totally, expecting Him to meet all of our needs. He told us in Philippians that He would supply all of our needs according to His riches in glory and I believed that He would come through for us because this was His idea. He had put it all together and so I was totally trusting in Him.

In Proverbs 3:6, the Bible says, "In all of our ways, acknowledge Him and He will direct our paths."

And in the fifth verse we are told that we must, "Trust in the Lord with all of thine heart and lean not unto thine own understanding."

I didn't know how He would provide, but my trust was completely in Him, and I knew our needs would be met. I remembered the story of God's people getting ready to cross the river Jordan to go into the Promised Land. The Bible tells us that the priests carrying the ark were instructed to step into the Jordan River. Even though the waters were high, they were told to step in. All the Israelites obeyed. And when they stepped in, the waters parted and they went across. I believed it was time for us to take the Lord at His word.

When you minister overseas it's not customary for the people you've come to serve to provide for you. Other times we have sent money ahead for our provisions. We knew that this time it would take a miracle, but we made a conscious decision, to totally trust in the Lord Jesus Christ that He would take care of us.

I thought of the story of Abraham, who was told by God to take his only son Isaac to Mount Moriah and offer him as not just a sacrifice, but a burnt offering unto the Lord. Early the next morning, Abraham took Isaac and, when they arrived at the foot of the mountain, Isaac said to his father, "We have the wood and the fire, but where is the sacrifice?"

Abraham said, "The Lord will provide the sacrifice." Then he told his servant, "We will return."

I believe that, as they were going up one side of the mountain, the Lord had the ram coming up the other side. Abraham couldn't see it then, but had faith in his heart that God somehow would provide for them to return. That's the kind of faith that we should have in the Lord. We don't always have that kind of faith, but God wants to build a greater faith in our lives. When they reached the top of the mountain, Abraham bound his son, put him on the altar was ready to bring the knife down to slay him.

The Lord stayed his hand and said, "Do not harm him, for now that I know your heart I know that you will hold nothing back from me."

Abraham lifted up his eyes, saw the ram caught in the thicket and knew for sure that the Lord had provided the sacrifice. I'm sure it was a great day of praising God, for Abraham obeyed the Lord and offered the best that he had. And the Lord gave him back his son. **Abraham passed the test**! I am sure they rejoiced all the way down Mount Moriah and rejoiced all the way home for what the Lord had done. So on that plane, my heart was full of faith, believing that God had put all of these meetings together. I had nothing to do with it. Therefore, He was going to provide somehow.

We arrived in Athens, Greece, where we had a wonderful meeting. God blessed in outstanding ways. We saw many saved, many healed from cancer, demons were cast out and people were delivered from bondage. There were only about 20 people in the church that first night and some were slain in the Spirit—a phenomenon they had never seen in Greece. The news of the glorious miracles that happened on that first night spread.

The next evening, the missionary interpreter came to pick us up in the hotel where we were staying and take us to the church. Since in Greece, the Greek Orthodox Church is the only denomination that is allowed to have buildings that look like churches, this Full Gospel church was meeting in a building on the fifth floor. When we walked into the church, the missionary was startled for a moment. He said to me, "We must be in the wrong place. We've never had this many people!"

They had opened the side wings of the church and were cleaning out the balcony that had never been used. Because people heard that miracles were happening, pastors and people from other churches had begun coming to our meetings.

We were scheduled to close on Wednesday night, but God blessed in such a powerful way, the pastors requested I stay longer. I told them I was scheduled to be with the pastor in Macedonia the next night. But that pastor was with us at this meeting and he said, "Oh my, brother. We have never seen anything like this in Greece in our lifetimes." God is moving in such a way that it must not be interrupted. Please stay here until Friday night and then we will take the bus to Macedonia for services this weekend."

We continued ministering until Friday and the service did not close until past 11 p.m. People stayed, even though the city busses stopped running at 10. The power of God was moving in salvation, healing and prophecy and many were filled with the Holy Spirit.

On that last evening, the pastors in charge said, "We are going to do something we have never done in the 50-year history of this church. We are going to take an offering for an American!" God blessed and rewarded us in a wonderful way, because we received a very generous offering. We then ministered in other cities in Greece and Macedonia and continued on to Israel, India and Sri Lanka.

CHAPTER SEVENTEEN

※

Forsaking Buddha

We prepared ourselves for a culture shock as we traveled to Bombay, Calcutta and Madras, India. We readied ourselves to recognize the demonic spirits that rule over that part of the world. We do not have room in this book to express how the extreme poverty and spiritual darkness reigning there affected us. And yet we were also heartened and inspired by the dedicated work of people like Mother Teresa and Mark and Hulda Buntain.

We found ourselves on a journey to Colombo, Sri Lanka, a major city on that island. We ministered in the evangelistic center there. God blessed in a wonderful way as we ministered in the Sunday services. On Monday morning, along with the pastor, associate pastor and about 20 of their young people, we traveled 120 miles south to Tangalle.

The pastor had been able to set up this crusade, since he knew the district judge of the area, who was an evangelical. He and the judge had made all the arrangements for the open-air meeting, setting up the platform, the sound, the lighting and so forth. Had it not been for the district judge, this crusade could not have happened, because this area was 99 percent Buddhist.

As we approached the city gates, there was an extremely large statue of Buddha that towered above the gate. My interpreter told me that, as far as he knew, the gospel had never been preached here and that he was so excited that this was happening during his lifetime.

The first night, the people crowded around the platform, awaiting our arrival. We were told that they had all walked to the crusade, some from 20 miles or more. The service started as young people ascended the platform and sang. The crowded audience had never heard anointed singing and worshipping Jesus. In fact, everything that was happening was totally foreign to them. God began to touch them in wonderful ways.

I was anointed to preach the simple message, knowing this was the first time they had ever heard. I began telling them about our great God; how He created the heavens and the Earth and made Adam and Eve and everything else on the earth. They listened intently as I told them how God's first children brought sin into the world, causing all to become sinners. I continued on, speaking in a very simplistic way, leading them on to the introduction of our Lord Jesus Christ and God the Father, who provided a way for our sins to be forgiven through His Son. I explained how Jesus had to die so we all could be delivered from our sins and any work of evil in our lives. And I told them how He is now alive and His power saves, delivers and heals us.

As I preached, I understood that, in order for these people to heed the call to bring Christ into their lives, they must first forsake Buddha. As a result, they would be excommunicated from their religion, separated from their families and would likely lose their jobs. To forsake Buddha required a significant price.

We began to pray for the sick and call out healings as the Lord led, and we began to see a great response from those who had been deaf and mute from birth. I would call them up and pray for them, we would snap our fingers and they would respond. Then the interpreter would tell them to repeat the word "áwma" which means "momma" and they would repeat the word several times.

They had been delivered from the deaf and dumb spirits and were healed. The Buddhist priests who were in the crowd would come and would take them alongside the platform after their healing, checking them and testing them. We saw the priests were becoming very disturbed, as many were being healed and accepting Jesus as their Savior every night.

A woman came who was stooped over with her head down to her knees. I thought of the woman in the Bible who was bent over and Jesus healed her. So I prayed for this deformed woman and slowly she stood upright. Much to our surprise, we saw that she was actually very tall – about 5'8". Everyone was amazed. Tangalle was a city of only about twenty thousand, so many who knew her were filled with wonder, because they were astonished that God had totally healed her. It was so exhilarating to see so many people miraculously healed. God gets all the glory, for He is the one who did it.

One night I saw police milling around the crowd. There were many men dressed in white with their arms folded, glaring at me. They were stationed in various places and their presence really seemed to disturb the leaders of our meeting. But we proceeded with the meeting and God continued to bless and heal the people.

As the meeting closed a few nights later, my interpreter, who was pastor of the church in Colombo, said to me, "I just can't thank you enough for your ministry in this crusade. It has been a dream of mine for 20 years to plant a church here."

We had made prior arrangements for his associate pastor to remain there and we had rented a building where he could live and hold regular services. Consequently, the Sunday after the meeting closed, those who had been converted and healed could come to learn more about their newfound faith. Before Betty and I left, we met with them in the new church building and taught them about water baptism, the baptism of the Holy Spirit, and we partook of Communion together. Our burden was not just to hold a successful crusade, but to know that through the funds we would send, this church would be established and would thrive. We were extremely excited and grateful to God.

My interpreter was also very happy that I had begun praying and believing for miracles on the very first night. He explained that most other ministers who come from the states take a night or so to build the people's faith. He then told me that a plan had been put in place to kill me.

I was shocked. And I asked him to tell me more.

"Did you notice the police and the men dressed in white who were in the crowd the other night?" he asked.

"Yes," I told him. "I wondered who they were and why they were there."

He said the men dressed in white were Buddhist priests. Their plan was to have me dance on the platform by the power of Buddha. And when this happened, it would be the sign that Buddha had delivered me into their hands. At that time they were to rush the platform and instantly kill me!

"Why didn't you tell me about this if you knew the plan?" I asked as calmly as I could manage.

"I knew that the power in you was greater than the power of Buddha," he explained simply. "So their plan could never work."

I thought more about the strange thing that happened to me that night. During the time the young people were singing, I had heard a distinct voice in my spirit telling me to get up and dance in a circle. I envisioned a Native American war dance with my fists in the air, chanting, "God is great! God is great!"

Even though this continued coming to me quite vividly and forcefully, I knew it was not from God and dismissed it from my mind. I was totally amazed that the power of Buddha had been strong enough to invade my mind.

My interpreter told me that through demonic faith and power in Buddha, they occasionally get miracles. The devil knew that I had danced holding hands in a circle with a group of pastors in Greece as we joyfully worshipped the Lord. He thought he could use this phenomenon to deliver me into the hands of Buddha. The Bible says,

"My sheep know me and they hear my voice." Thankfully I discerned the voice I heard was not God's.

It really is beneficial to know the voice of God. We need to recognize the spirits of darkness today in the church even in America.

We rejoiced that God had protected us. We rejoiced that he saved, healed and blessed the people. About a year after our crusade, a young pastor who started a church in a nearby village was brutally murdered in the presence of his wife and children. Hallelujah, the work of the Lord still stands today and we pray for the Christian people, the pastors and the churches in that region. Only eternity will tell all the wonderful things the Lord accomplished in that crusade.

We left that place rejoicing and continued our mission around the world. At the halfway point in our journey, we stopped to minister in Singapore and Malaysia. In Singapore, I prayed for a little four-year-old girl who had never walked. After prayer, she began walking and running back to me. As I have said before, there is not enough space in this book to relate all our travels and experiences in the Lord's work.

We were treated royally in Taiwan. General Woo and his secretary came to the airport to meet us and, by the slight of his hand it seemed, we flew through customs. We were guests at the Grand Hotel where all the dignitaries stay. And as guests of General Woo, we were treated to a nine-course meal in a beautiful private room. God allowed me to minister to an elderly missionary woman who had given her life in service there. She was overwhelmed that the Lord told someone she had never met of her most secret desires, and then assured her they would come to pass.

When we arrived back in San Diego from the ministry around the world, I still had a $20 bill in my pocket. God had met our every need in abundance, for we even had enough to stop in Hawaii for two days!

CHAPTER EIGHTEEN

❦

Supernatural Provision

Prior to our ministry trip around the world, the Lord told me to sell my antique Ford Model A. I was a little reluctant in my flesh, but I knew to obey God. So I said goodbye to my beautiful Model A, which had been restored and was in beautiful condition. I knew God would sell it and, almost immediately after advertising it, a buyer came and paid almost four times what I had paid some years before.

God was going to use this as seed money to prime our trip around the world. And after all, I've found it's best to obey what the Lord says to do. There are no regrets that way. The Lord has provided in an almost unbelievable, magnanimous way, and Betty and I know that God was and is able to provide more than we could ask or could have anticipated early in our lives together.

Whatever the Lord says, do it immediately. When the wine ran out at the wedding feast, Mary, the mother of Jesus, told the servants to do whatever her son told them to do. Jesus instructed them to fill the wine pots with water. They obeyed and His first miracle resulted in the best wine for the wedding guests. In our day, He still works miracles to meet our needs.

Very early in my life the Lord taught me to walk in obedience. I have found He requires you to do just what He says, when He says it. Otherwise, you might reach His plan partially ... but not totally.

For example, one time while traveling, conducting a motor home ministry, we were driving in Montana and passed a church on the highway. The Lord told me to turn around because He wanted me to minister to the pastor of that church. I remember feeling drawn to it as we passed, but I didn't see a name or denominational sign. The first chance I got, I started looking for a place to turn our rig around. Since we were towing our car, this wasn't an easy task. Eventually though, we managed to turn around and get back to the church. I found the pastor in his office, introduced myself and told him that the Lord had told me to come and minister to him. I remember how delighted he was with every word from the Lord. The large offering I gave him met needs that I knew nothing about. God was teaching me to obey and I'm glad that I acted in His timing.

While ministering once in Kauai, Hawaii, we drove past a church with a tent on the property and thought perhaps they were having a tent revival. The Lord spoke to me and told me to go back and minister to the pastor. We drove back to the church property and asked to speak with the pastor. When we were taken to his office, we introduced ourselves and I explained that I was there to minister and encourage him.

I told him, "The Lord knows that you and the church have gone through the greatest spiritual tornado that you have ever known. The enemy has been coming in like a flood with hurricane-force winds. But God wants you to know that He is with you and the church will succeed and be blessed as never before!"

I could tell this news was a tremendous blessing to him because, as I was speaking, he began to fall to his knees. Then he fell flat on his face and began sobbing. He told us that a few months prior, they had experienced a literal hurricane on the island that had caused considerable damage to the property. At the same time, the church was experiencing a devastating spiritual storm, which seemed insurmountable. We gave him a $100 bill, feeling so privileged to have been blessed ourselves and knowing unmistakably that we had blessed him.

He invited me to minister in his church, but we had no time on that trip. We made arrangements to come the following year, and the Lord used us in a wonderful way. That church was blessed abundantly.

There was another time in our new ministry when God was teaching us complete obedience as we walked by faith. I went to a large department store to purchase a drill. The clerk charged me $15 less than the shelf price. I was thankful for the bargain price and proceeded to put it out of my mind. However, the Lord began to deal with me, saying He wanted me to go back and pay the stated shelf price. I didn't understand His reasoning, because I thought it was most likely just on sale. I kept trying to put God's charge out of my mind, but God kept troubling me to obey.

So the next day I returned to the store and told them I wanted to pay the full price for the drill. They told me not to worry about it; the drill was on sale when I bought it. I hesitated when I looked at the shelf and saw that the drill wasn't on sale. But they assured me that even though the drill was not on sale presently, the computer showed it had been at the sale price on the day I made the purchase. As I drove back home, the Lord continued to disturb my peace and instructed me to go back and pay full price. I tried to reason with Him but He said, "I want you to pay the full amount for it. Obey me, not what they are telling you to do."

I returned to the store and this time I asked to speak to the manager. He also assured me I had paid the correct price on the day of my purchase. I left again, but the Lord continued to disquiet me over the next six days saying, "I told you to pay the shelf price. Are you obeying man or me? I want you to do what I say, not what they say."

I finally realized this was a mandatory act of obedience required by the Lord. So I returned again, taking the $15 to the first cashier. I explained to her unequivocally that the Lord told me to pay the regular price on this drill and I laid the cash by her register and walked out. I decided that no one would have occasion or time to change my mind. The Lord was teaching me to have **total obedience**, doing what He requires, not what others say.

This ordeal seemed almost ridiculous. But without doubt, this is what He required of me. Never again was I troubled with the price of that drill. Over the years I have often used that drill. Each time I'm reminded that the Lord taught me a valuable lesson of obedience. You can find peace only when you obey the Lord.

Pleasing the Lord through simple obedience is the most significant thing I can do. I know there is coming a day in my not-too-far distant future, when He will say, "Well done, my good and faithful servant." I live for that most crucial day by living my life now in the light of eternity.

The Lord may have you in His oven, turning up the heat. You may say, "God, I don't understand why I'm going through these things." You may say, "I don't know what you are trying to teach me, for you seem so far off."

He is preparing you for the work that He has for you to do. Don't be discouraged, because the pressures of this world are nothing and are not to be compared to the splendor and glories that are to come. Even in this life, we experience glory when we allow the Lord to use and work through us. I urge you to surrender totally to the Lord. Pray much, fast, seek His face and let God direct your steps.

The Bible says the Lord directs the steps of a good person. So even if you don't understand His commands, do what He tells you to do, when He tells you to do it. His plans for you are for your good and not for evil. Trust Him and know that as high as the heavens are above the earth, so are His ways and thoughts above yours. The Word tells us obedience is better than sacrifice, so be obedient to Him and He will greatly reward and use you.

CHAPTER NINETEEN

✖

Three Pastors in Victoria

In 1992, we ministered in British Columbia. On our way, we traveled up the West Coast from San Diego, stopping in several cities to minister along the way. We attended Sunday services at a church in Washington, near the Canadian border. After church, the Lord spoke to me, telling me that He wanted me to go to Vancouver Island. But I didn't understand why. I mentioned it to my wife and she said she would love to go, since she'd heard it was beautiful. She was especially excited about seeing the city of Victoria.

We put our car on the ferry and when we arrived on the island we headed toward the city – all the time wondering what the Lord 's purpose was for us there. We stopped and went through the beautiful Buschard Gardens, then proceeded on the main highway to Victoria. We booked a hotel and had dinner and, since Betty especially likes historical settings, we walked around downtown and drove around the city, taking in some wonderful sites.

Foremost on my mind was listening for the Lord to reveal His purpose for our being there. After a good night's rest I was in prayer when the Lord spoke to me and said, "I want you to call three ministers on this island and I will give them a word through you."

I didn't know any ministers or pastors in the area, but He instructed me to have my wife take the phone book and choose three pastors. At first she was a bit apprehensive, thinking this was weird. But I assured her the Lord said she would choose the right ones.

Betty picked three pastors. I called the first one, introduced myself and explained that the Lord wanted me to give him a word of encouragement. When I ministered to him, he was really receptive and seemed to be pleased and blessed. He told me if I ever planned to return to the island I should get in touch, because he would like for me to minister in his church.

The second pastor was also blessed and gladly accepted my words from the Lord especially for him. Just as with the first, he thanked me and asked me to minister if we ever returned.

The scriptural reference God gave me for the third pastor was Hebrews 13:5, "I will not in any way fail you or give you up, nor leave you without support. I will not, I will not, I will not in any degree leave you helpless nor forsake or let you down or relax my hold on you, assuredly not."

As I related God's word, the pastor began to weep and asked, "Oh my brother, is there any way I can meet with you? Would you stay on hold while I call my wife and see if we could have you for lunch?" We excitedly agreed.

We found the home and were 20 minutes early, so I decided to drive along the east shore that was close to their home. As we were driving, I looked to my left and saw a minister friend, Willard Cantelon whom I've known for many years, sitting on his porch.

I had no idea that he lived on this island and Betty didn't think it could possibly be him. But I was positively sure. I turned around and pulled up in front of his house. When we climbed out of the car, he recognized us. It had been many, many years since we had been together, but it was wonderful to see him. We talked for a brief time, reminiscing on God's goodness to us all. He blessed us with his latest publication and told us he felt directly impressed to sit on his front porch that day.

In fact, that was the first time he'd sat on that porch in the five years he had lived there. We all concluded it was a God-arranged encounter, allowing us to fellowship with this precious brother. It was a paramount gift thrown into our pathway for our obedience to the Lord.

At the third pastor's home we enjoyed a delicious lunch and conversation. "There's no way you could know this," he told us, "but when you called, I had just concluded a phone conversation with my church treasurer, who gave me devastating news. Our church treasury is in the red about twenty-one thousand dollars.

"I couldn't believe it, but he explained that a number of our church people who recently visited a former communist country have come home burdened for the many needs they saw. They've decided to take their tithes and, instead of giving them to the church, use them to purchase food and supplies for that country.

"So, when you called, I knew it was God," he concluded.

The pastor told us he had no training in the ministry and was not comfortable preaching about money and tithing. He explained he had been an attorney in this city for several years before being compelled to pastor this church without the benefit of pastoral training.

The Lord enabled me to teach him about how to minister to the people on tithing, which is God's plan for supporting a local church. We then prayed that God would give him supernaturally ability to teach His plan, so the local church could be blessed. He was so grateful we had come, believing it was a divine appointment, and he invited us to come and minister at a later time. It was a great blessing for us to be used by God in Victoria in the lives of these three pastors and to renew our love for an old friend.

CHAPTER TWENTY

✖

A Primary Church

In 1983, after traveling supernaturally for nine years, God began to show me that we were going to pastor a church again. During these years, we had many offers to pastor, however, I didn't feel any of these particular places were in alignment with God's will for our lives. In 1977 and again in 1980, the Lord brought prophecies from two well-know men of God to our minds.

The first prophesy left us somewhat perplexed concerning the following revelation: "For as Nehemiah, you have the vision of that which is torn down. You are ready for that which shall open and know that as this opportunity has opened it is well in your hands. But you will build upon your foundation that I have given and you will build upon the foundation that, yea, the anointing of the Lord will bring to pass within you. There's just a wonderful opportunity that, Hallelujah, the Lord is going to seemingly clean the situation up and prepare for your ministry. Don't worry about the finances, for everything will flow together. You will have a real settling place. It will open up for you perfectly!"

An excerpt from the second prophecy given said: "There is a multiplication of ministries that God has thrust into your life. You won't feel that I'm out here alone and that my brothers do not understand me because you'll know that God has made you like a prophet of old, a consoler. The Lord is going to bring you into a body and you will be established as an apostle and pastor to the believers. Ministers will come to you for council and even in secret and in the nighttime. You will have wisdom and answers for them. There'll be times that you will be like a father to other ministers. You won't even feel important, but through your life, Jesus will minister to the questions they have unanswered. His answers."

During all our traveling was hidden in my heart the promise from God, given in 1975, that He would bless me and there would be one primary church that would support our ministry financially. The two prophecies given seemed to be strongly confirming that promise.

In early 1983, I felt strongly led to attend a church in San Diego on a Sunday morning. After the service was over, my wife and I were walking to the parking lot and I was groaning in my spirit. "Honey what's wrong?" Betty asked.

"I don't want to talk about it," I replied.

Of course she continued to quiz me, so I told her the Lord let me know that the pastor of this church was living in adultery. "I don't know why God told me these things," I said. "I really can't do anything about it. I guess I can pray for him."

About 10 months later, I received a phone call from a man who introduced himself as one of the pastors of that same church. He informed me the senior pastor had resigned and he wanted to know if I would be interested in considering the pastorate of the church. I knew none of the people in that church, and I didn't know him. But he told me later that he attended a service where we had ministered in the area sometime back. Before discussing this invitation further, I asked for a few weeks to pray over the matter.

When we met a few weeks later, he explained that had been a nominal church that didn't believe in the baptism of the Holy Spirit with the evidence of speaking in tongues. But while he and his wife were in the mission field representing this denomination, they had received the Holy Spirit with the evidence of other tongues. When they returned to the states, they were assigned to this particular church and it had grown to became one of the largest independent charismatic churches in the San Diego area during the late sixties and seventies.

Then he told us of the long list of challenges we would face. To make a long story short, we became the pastors of that church. It was almost totally unbelievable! What God had shown me almost a year earlier was reality, for the head deacon's wife was carrying around a baby who had been fathered by the former pastor.

Surely God had placed me there to fulfill His promise that He was going to bless me with one primary church which would support our ministry financially. Both of the prophecies had been completely fulfilled.

During my seven years of pastoring there, God did great things. Many miracles and healings happened and all the gifts of the spirit flowed freely. The happenings during our ministry there would fill another book!

I continued to minister in traveling at times, while Betty cared for the ministry and operation of the church. The congregation was faithful to pray and financially support us as we were called out in full-time traveling ministry again in 1991. Oh yes, I wanted the financial security to come sooner, but one thing I've learned in these many years is that God is sometimes very close, but He is never late. The people in this church have been a blessing to our financial needs and in many other ways for over 22 years. Our God is faithful to accomplish His promises!

CHAPTER TWENTY-ONE

❧

Ministering in a Motor Home

At the time we were led to leave the pastorate there, the Lord directed us to purchase a motor home. While making a covenant with Him in 1975, He assured us the day would come when we would have a motor home. God worked out all the details and we began to travel, ministering in churches, men's advances, tent meetings and wherever God would lead us. He opened many doors and we would be gone in ministry for up to five months at a time.

We traveled and ministered from the West to the East Coast, in Mexico and in Canada. God blessed us tremendously and accomplished many outstanding miracles. Due to our steady income, we were able to bless many pastors. We bought washers, dryers, other essential articles and gave special offerings to those we felt were in need or just needed to be blessed. Many times we returned the honorariums they gave from the offerings they received for us as we felt the Lord was saying they were in a pivotal time of need.

We kept pressing on toward the mark for the prize of the high calling of God in Christ Jesus as in Philippians 3:14, for we believed greater things were yet to come. Hebrews 10:35-36 tells us, "Cast not away your confidence which has great recompense of reward, for you have need of patience that after you have done the will of God you might receive the promise."

We simply kept believing and trusting in the Lord, knowing that His word is true. Many stop too soon, but we should have in our hearts the philosophy to never, never, never give up! God will fulfill His promise if we will walk in His will and His plan in obedience.

We rejoiced once more as we remembered the prophesy from 1975, where we were told we would be liberators, would be greatly used in the last day revival, would find an open path into the historic denominations, would be refiners of the breech, would build up the Tabernacle of David (praise) and bring **new life** to old places. The prophecy in 1977 was mostly fulfilled to the letter when I became pastor in 1984.

"You will lead many," said the latter part of the prophecy, "and your ministry shall be turned to the shepherds that hover around the fire, not knowing the mysteries of the darkness. You have an anointing to stir up my shepherds for this hour, and touch many and encourage them at this hour. This will be a mystery, but it will happen."

The prophecy I received in 1980 was also fulfilled in part when I became pastor. "Ministers will come to you for counsel and even in secret and in the nighttime. You will have wisdom and answers for them, there will be times that you'll be like a father to other ministers. You won't feel important, but through your life, Jesus will minister to the questions that they have unanswered – His answers."

During the years of pastoring in San Diego, God used another pastor friend and me to direct a ministry called "San Diego for Jesus." Sometimes we met at his church and sometime at our church. We held a monthly meeting for all the area ministers where they could fellowship, share and pray together. We also sponsored large rallies, bringing in well-know speakers and all the churches would participate. This was very successful and met a tremendous need in the lives of pastors.

Now as we traveled in the motor home, ministering, we continued to minister to pastors and found both of these amazing prophecies were fulfilled to the letter. Many times I would have pastors who were seeking answers pick my brain until wee hours of the morning. Many times while I was sharing with them, I could see that they desperately needed a spiritual father. One pastor tried to persuade me to park the motor home in his church parking lot and stay for six months, for he felt such a crucial need of godly wisdom from a spiritual father. Another, whose father went to heaven very early in his life, has been in contact down through the years whenever he needs counsel.

Betty and I also found the references in these prophecies were amazingly correct when referring to ministering in historic denominations. We ministered in Baptist churches, in Lutheran churches, in the basement of a Catholic church, in Foursquare, Church of God, Pentecostal Church of God, Pentecostal Holiness and innumerable nondenominational, charismatic and Assemblies of God Churches.

These are just a very few of the many marvelous ways that God used and directed us during the years since we were called out of the pastorate in 1975. God may be doing similar things through many of you as you walk with the Lord and are obedient to him. If you are His sheep, who know His voice, do whatever He says for you to do, without questioning. We continue to want to be a blessing wherever God sends us. We still stand on the Word in Jeremiah 1:7, "I will send you where I want you to go and I will put my words in your mouth." And it happens just as He promised.

Remember how God provided for Elijah when he was obedient, and how he went to King Ahab and told him there would be no rain or dew until he said it would happen. For several years there was no moisture at all. And yet God provided for His servant. God sent him down to the brook Cherith with a water supply and the beaks of ravens brought food.

Betty and I have proven that God provides over and over. God has taken care of us when it appeared impossible. The experiences I share are meant to encourage you not to lean on your ability to understand, but to trust in the Lord with all your heart.

You may be facing similar circumstances, but He has everything under control and will provide for you. When God speaks to you, the provision for what He has asked you to achieve will be there. He will not fail and He is in the process of teaching you to **walk supernaturally**.

God provided water, manna and quail from heaven for millions of his people as they wandered through the desert. Their clothes and shoes did not wear out for 40 years, for God supernaturally took care of them. When Moses died, God instructed them to cross the Jordan River under the leadership of Joshua.

God spoke to Joshua, telling him to take the people across the river Jordan into the land of their inheritance. But before they went across the river, at the hill of foreskins, those who had not previously been circumcised had to submit to the sharp knife.

Likewise, God is circumcising our hearts even this day. He is preparing us to tenderly hear His voice. Consequently, when He says it's time to go forth, we will be ready to follow His instructions. Stand fast, be strong, be courageous and then rise up. For His glory will be manifested through you. He is decidedly preparing you for that which is on the horizon when His glory will be revealed through you.

It most often happened that the night before we were to leave for a ministry trip, we were still trying to find provisions. In the natural, God does use people to meet our need. We remained steadfast, unmovable, with our trust in our God. I recall many times on the last possible evening, He would send people to our home, bringing us money, sometimes as much as $1,000.

One time a friend called and said, "Oh, I'm glad you are still home! The Lord has told me that I am to bring you some money. What's going on?"

I explained that we were leaving in the morning for a ministry tour. God moved in so many outstanding and phenomenal ways to provide for us over the years. We can only share a portion in print, trusting they will provoke you to also desire a **supernatural walk** with Him.

Another time I was talking to the Lord in prayer. I asked Him to let me know if we were still on target. I prayed that, if we were, would he confirm this by providing a large offering, which was essential at that time. Since we were still under orders never to say anything to anyone concerning our needs, they were addressed solely to the Lord, our provider.

The next evening we were not ministering and decided to attend church where they were not familiar with our ministry or us. During the service, the Lord spoke to the pastor and told him they were supposed to take an offering for us. We had just met Him and were only slightly acquainted with two or three people from this church. So he announced that he was receiving the offering for the Skinners' ministry and the Lord said it was to be $1,000. And if that specific amount didn't come in during the offering they would add from the treasury to achieve that total.

This was an amazing act of faith and obedience for that pastor, especially since it was rather a small Sunday night service with primarily younger people. How amazing is our God? We ask one day and He answers the next evening. In all probability, this doesn't happen often, because God does not operate on our time clock.

As we prepared for one of our motor home ministry trips, we had particular needs. So I asked the Lord to provide a large offering in an uncommon, unusual way. While on our journey, I checked my messages and found one from a man who wanted to send an offering. He left his name, asking me how and where he could send the check. I asked Betty if she knew who this man was, but neither of us could place him. I called back and spoke to him and he sent a check for $1,000.

When I called to thank him, I asked how he knew of our ministry. "Have you been in some of the services?"

He said he didn't know us. So I asked, "Then what prompted you to send us an offering?"

Much to our amazement he replied, "The Lord spoke to me and told me to look in the yellow pages and He would show me someone I was to bless. When I saw your name, I knew you were the one He wanted to have my offering, so I left the message on your phone."

"By the way," he said, "I will be sending you more."

We were once more amazed that God heard and answered our request so specifically. God is clearly so on target because what is the possibility of this happening once? Or ever again? We rejoiced for this great provision. This man, whom we had never met and have never heard from again, lavishly sent us a total of $4,500! God is faithful to provide. You can trust Him. It's in the bank.

The key is to obey God and move toward obedience with what He says to do. Then have faith in God to answer. He will not fail you. Betty maintains to this day that we reaped the $4,500 harvest because we were obedient in Victoria when we followed the peculiar command of the Lord to pick three pastors from the yellow pages and give them the word of the Lord!

The scripture says, "And Jesus went about all the cities and villages, teaching in their synagogues. There He preached the gospel of the kingdom, and healed every sickness and disease among the people." Matthew 9:35

Luke 6:19 tells us, "And the whole multitude sought to touch Him, for there went virtue out of Him and healed them all."

In Hebrews 13:8 we learn, "Jesus Christ the same yesterday and today and forever."

He desires great miracles, signs and wonders, but we must yield to Him. We need to step out in faith and confidence, believing He will do these miracles. He cannot do the miracles unless we exercise faith in Him.

I Peter 2:24 says, "He bore our sins in His own body on the tree, that we, being dead to sins, should live unto righteousness by whose stripes ye were healed."

I want you to rise up, swell up in faith and believe God to do the impossible. He is a God who is able to do it today just as He did it many years ago. The Bible teaches us that, without faith, it is impossible to please God.

In Mark 11:22, Jesus says, "Have faith in God." If we will not open our mouth and exercise faith, He cannot accomplish these things He wants to do. The scripture teaches us we can operate in faith by simply believing in God.

Remember the story in Matthew 17, after Jesus, Peter, James and John came down from the Mount of Transfiguration? They found a man who had with him a child who suffered from seizures and, as a result, had fallen into the fire and into the water several times.

The man said to Jesus, "I brought him unto thy disciples, and they could not cure him."

"Then Jesus answered and said, 'Oh faithless and perverse generation, how long shall I be with you? How long shall I suffer with you? Bring him hither to me.' Then Jesus simply rebuked the devil and the devil went out of him and the child was cured from that very hour."

We can learn that we don't have to grunt and groan, but rather simply speak the word of God in faith and in the name of Jesus. Jesus dealt directly with the devil, for he was obviously trying to kill and destroy the child; casting him into the fire and into the water. The child was totally healed and made normal when Jesus spoke the word.

The disciples asked Jesus, "Why couldn't we cast the devil out?"

"And Jesus said unto them, 'Because of your unbelief: for verily I say unto you, If ye have faith as a grain of mustard seed, ye shall say unto this mountain, Remove hence to yonder place; and it shall remove; and nothing shall be impossible unto you.' "

I don't know if you've ever seen a mustard seed, but it's awfully small. It is so tiny it looks like a period at the end of a sentence. Jesus said if you would have that much faith, you could move the mountain. You tell the mountain to be moved and it will be moved. God wants to move the mountains in our lives as we exercise faith.

There is something we have to do; we just have to have faith in God. God will do the work if we have faith and will just step out and believe Him and trust Him. Nothing is impossible with Him. He wants us to do the greater works, but it cannot be done unless we have radical faith. God, give us radical faith!

CHAPTER TWENTY-TWO

✖

Divine Healing

There have been many times in my life when the Lord has touched my body. He provides not only for our salvation and peace in our souls, He also provides healing for our bodies as we walk in victory with our Lord Jesus Christ. Our bodies haven't been redeemed yet, but the time is coming when we will have no more sickness, disease, pain, heartache or sorrow. However, in this life we have still have to battle against sickness and disease and strive to walk in divine health.

In the beginning of this book I shared my parents' testimony of when I was born a hydrocephalic child – water-head baby. After they took me to church and prayed for me, liquid instantly began to discharge out of an ear. God miraculously, supernaturally, through the power of the name of Jesus, healed and restored me and within a couple of days my head was absolutely normal. That was over 80 years ago, so I thank God, for I know that I wouldn't be alive today without divine intervention.

If my parents hadn't believed with faith in their hearts that God would heal me, and hadn't taken me to the man of God, the pastor of the church, then he and the church would not have prayed in simple faith for me and God could not have healed me.

I've had several incidents my lifetime which have brought me face to face with death. When I was about 12 years old, I had a very serious crisis with my left ear. Doctors said the condition had been developing since I was a toddler and I often had infections. I can remember having excruciating pain in that ear many times. They said that, since it was not taken care of when I was young, much of the tissue had been destroyed in the mastoid area. They wondered if I would live through the operation, because they would be working with nerves very close to the brain and they could not ensure my parents that my face would not be disfigured. But because of faith and prayer, God kept me alive and has restored me. I have no disfigured face and have been marvelously blessed all these years!

When I fell at age 16, I was told I was facing death. I had broken my back, tailbone, ribs and hip, as well as smashing a vertebrae. Plus, my kidneys weren't functioning. The prognosis for recovery was grim. But through His love and mercy, God had a plan and a purpose for my life. He raised me up and healed me completely. The doctors and the nurses were amazed when I walked out of that hospital within 30 days. Thanks be unto the Lord my God.

About 30 years later I was diagnosed with Multiple Sclerosis. Just after the diagnosis, a pastor friend happened to come by for a visit. He laid hands on me and prayed for me in the hospital bed. Praise God, today there are no signs of Multiple Sclerosis in my body.

In 1993, I had prostate cancer and God brought me through that time of facing death. Now it is many years later and I have no sign of cancer in my body. Praise the Lord!

In February 1999, I was stricken down with a stroke. I want to share this testimony in a little more detail. After attending the Sunday morning service, as I was standing in the lobby, I began having some indications that I could be having a stroke. That afternoon, I checked into the hospital and they confirmed it was a stroke. I was cognizant and communicating without slurred speech, but I often felt odd, as if I might pass out. As time progressed I found myself in a room in the intensive care unit. My wife, daughter and brother were there. praying for my healing and believing that I would walk out of the hospital in the morning.

Later that night I began to feel a tingling in my right side. Then I felt kind of a twitching in my right side. Later still I felt the tingling and the twitching and was aware of a jerking in my right side. The nurse called my doctor at 1 a.m. He instructed her to take me for a head scan to see if they could see bleeding in my brain. I remember having the brain scan and then returning to my room in the elevator. Then I lost consciousness.

The next morning when I awoke, I realized that I was paralyzed on my right side. Nothing was moving, not even a twitch from a little finger and my speech was very slurred. I began to pray, "God I didn't think you were through with me yet! God you've got to help me!"

After praying this way for about 20 minutes, I began to question God, wondering what was happening in my body. Hearing nothing, I began to conclude that maybe my life and my ministry were over. I began to get excited, thinking I might soon see my Lord and Savior face to face. I began to worship and praise Him saying, "Oh I'm longing to see you, Lord Jesus."

Then the Lord spoke to me and distinctly said, "No, not yet! The devil meant this for evil. But I'm going to turn it for good. I'm going to raise you up and restore you. You will continue to travel in the motor home, going wherever I send you. I'm going to raise you up."

Immediately, I had to change gears. I had really been getting excited to see the Lord. But now that He had told me I was being healed and restored, my faith had to adjust to His word to me. The word of God doesn't say we have to have a world of faith. We just need a tiny mustard seed of faith. I knew that I had to put my little mustard seed of faith into action, believing His word that states, "I am the Lord thy God that healeth thee. Ask anything in my name and the Father will do it."

I acted on my faith immediately by calling out for a nurse. When she came, I asked her to lower the rails on my bed so I could get up and walk.

"Mr. Skinner, you cannot walk," she said. "You are totally paralyzed on the right side."

I explained to her that I realized my condition, but felt God was going to help me to walk! We argued back and forth until finally she walked away. I summoned another nurse, but the results were the same.

"Mr. Skinner, you don't realize the seriousness of your condition," the second nurse exclaimed. "You are totally paralyzed on the right side. **You cannot walk**!"

I told her I was completely aware of my physical condition, but the Lord was going to help me. She walked away. I was sure they thought I was not in my right mind. I prayed, hoping my wife would arrive soon.

Thinking I would be dismissed early, my wife called the hospital at 7 a.m. She was told that I had suffered a massive stroke, resulting in paralysis. Betty was shocked at their report and called our daughter Cyndi, who said was she taking our two grandsons out of school and they would arrive at the hospital, pronto.

When Betty arrived we talked briefly. Then I requested that she watch my feet, because I desperately wanted a little sign from the Lord. I exercised my faith and waited for the miracle to begin.

I was lying flat on my back and couldn't see my feet, so Betty watched as I attempted to wiggle my toes. In my mind I felt them moving… But she saw no movement, even when I asked her to look closer. I told her how frustrated I was with the nurses who denied my request to lower the rails. I asked Betty to find someone who would come and help me, because I needed to exercise my faith in God's word concerning my healing.

She found a physical therapist and explained to her that I wanted to get up and walk, and that I believed the Lord was going to help me. "I'm afraid you don't realize how serious this is," the physical therapist replied.

Betty quickly and strongly confirmed that we both understood my condition, but firmly believed the Lord would help me. She finally convinced the therapist to come to my room. Again, the therapist emphasized that I could not walk. And when I kept on insisting, she suddenly walked away.

But she returned soon, lowered the rails and helped me sit up on the bed. My head began to whirl and I thought I was going to pass out. "Are you sure you want try to walk, Mr. Skinner?" the physical therapist asked.

I assured her the answer was yes, so she put a belt around me and stood me up. With her help and the aid of a walker, I hobbled, nearly dragging myself to the foot of the bed and back. That day she returned two times and helped me to walk. I acted on my faith with everything that was within me.

The next morning I told both Betty and the physical therapist that I was going to walk to the door of my room and back three times that day. Initially the therapist tried to discourage me, just as she had done the day before. But with my insistence and the help of the Lord, I successfully achieved my goal and walked three times that day.

The next day I announced, "Today I'm going to walk down the hall and back."

This time the therapist replied, "Whatever you say, Reverend Skinner. Whatever you say. This is amazing – I've never seen anything like this. I'm excited and, if you want to try to walk to the end of the corridor and back, I'll get the belt and off we'll go!" She was thrilled, for she saw each day I was making progress, little by little.

I was grateful for the progress, but said to God, "Wouldn't it give you **more** glory, if this miracle could happen as it did in Acts 3? Why can't it be like it was with Peter and the man who had been lame since birth? Peter took the man by the hand and you immediately strengthened his feet and ankle bones and he got up, walking and leaping and praising God and causing a great stir in the temple.

"Lord, wouldn't that be better?" I asked. "I'll do the same thing if you will give me a great miracle like that." However, it appeared my miracle would show no resemblance to that of the lame man.

Little by little, the Lord, was guiding me to exercise faith and trust in Him. The therapist told my wife and my daughter she was excited to work with me, but there were plans to transfer me to another hospital where older citizens were comfortably allowed to vegetate until they died. She told us to talk to our doctor and persuade him to order that I stay in this hospital. They tried their best, but the doctor said there was no way my insurance would pay for another day there. So I was destined to be transferred the next morning. My doctor assured the family I would be in a great therapy program at the new hospital.

When I arrived, the staff reviewed my records. They read about the massive stroke and its result: my speech was slurred and the right side of my body was paralyzed. But they didn't realize that God was healing me. Even though it was difficult to explain, I kept on believing God and trusting Him. At first, the staff treated and spoke to me as if this stroke had just happened and I was totally helpless. They were very surprised when I exceeded their expectations.

As the days passed, God continued to help me. I got out of bed on my own, went to the bathroom alone and was able to adjust the thermostat on the wall. As God kept healing me, I would remind Him of every promise he had made to me, and nothing could circumvent my faith. My belief was constantly reinforced and, as each day went by, I improved more and more.

One day I went into an assembly room across the hall from my room where I noticed patients gathering together in fellowship. One woman told me she was in this hospital because she had attempted suicide.

"I won't fail next time," she told me, "because I'm going to get Doctor Kevorkian to help me."

I witnessed to her, telling her about Jesus and how much He loved her and how anxious He was to help her. She seemed receptive and allowed me to pray with her. When I saw her the next day, her entire attitude and appearance had changed. She looked lovely and had applied makeup and was wearing her jewelry. God used me in many ways while in this hospital, but space does not permit me to share more.

As the time passed, my progress was amazing. However, I had no control of the toes on my right foot, which made it difficult to walk. My toes actually hung down and dragged the floor as I walked. Two hospital personnel came to make a mold of my leg, ankle and foot so a plastic brace could be constructed to hold up my foot and toes as I walked.

After they left, I stood up as I was praying and declared that my foot and toes were healed in the name of Jesus. I said to the Lord, "I believed you when you said I would be healed and restored, so I believe I am **totally** healed and I will not have to wear that brace!" I took my left hand and kind of shook my right leg and said, "Leg, you will function properly and perfectly in the name of Jesus."

Two days later they returned with the fiberglass brace, remarking how nice it looked. And I agreed. Then they told me that they needed to try it on my foot. I completely ignored their request, arose from my bed normally and said, "Sorry fellows, you are too late. I don't need a brace, for God has healed me and my foot is perfect."

They were simply flabbergasted! They could not believe what they saw. They looked at their paperwork to see if they had the right room and the right man. God completely amazed those two men. Their regulations required them to see if it fit my foot. But I never wore it, because the Lord had healed me.

One day a nurse came in asking, "Have you noticed we are all fighting over you?"

"Yes," I said. "What's going on?"

"We are all fighting over you because we want a piece of the action," she said. "You make us look good. We don't ever have patients like you around here."

I thanked all of the staff for their help, but constantly reminded them that it was God who was healing and restoring me.

To make a long story shorter, I had been in both hospitals for a total of 15 days and, on the sixteenth day, I was released. The doctors and nurses were utterly amazed. It was a miracle that God had healed me. I was able to use my right hand, though I was walking slower and more cautiously. The staff suggested I still use the aid of a cane. But, much to my consternation, they wanted to wheel me out of the hospital to my daughter's car. I told them I would not get into that wheelchair, because I knew that was the exact place the enemy wanted me.

The staffed called the director of the hospital who simply said, "Oh if that is Mr. Skinner, just let him walk and make sure he gets to the car."

My daughter was driving and I told her to stop by the first hospital where I had been admitted. "Why do you need to go there?" she asked.

"I want to go back to that ICU floor and show them what the Lord has done!" I asserted.

Betty thought I was being a bit excessive. "Let's come back another time," she suggested.

But I would not take no for an answer. We went up the elevator and I walked to the ICU area, found a doctor who recognized me and said, "Look what the Lord has done!" I told everyone I saw who recognized me what the Lord had done.

As per the hospital and insurance policy, a physical therapist was sent to our home the next day. We had a very long hall, so she had me walk up and down and do several tasks. She just couldn't believe my abilities and asked, "Why did they send me here? You don't need me."

This was yet another opportunity to rejoice in the mighty healing power of God. I gave my testimony to everyone I met – to those who wanted to hear it and probably to just as many who didn't want to hear it! I remember that one pastor called me in the hospital a week after I had been admitted. He had heard about my stroke and suggested canceling a meeting we had scheduled in the near future.

My speech was still a bit slurred, but I said, "Oh no, God is going to totally heal me and I'll be there. I will not miss one meeting where I am scheduled to speak."

God loved and honored my faith, and I went to that meeting, which was several hundred miles away, and then we went to a camp meeting. And I also shared in a church in the same area. I have never hesitated to share with people this great miracle that the Lord did in my life. I give him praise, honor and glory. It is Jesus who has done the work. We need to keep on believing God, for He is able to do more than we could ask or think. It has been over 11 years since this miracle. God continues to use me as I exercise my faith; doing miracles, signs and wonders as I am ministering in the states or abroad.

I want to encourage you to have faith just the size of a mustard seed in a great big, awesome God. Exercise the faith that you have! Jesus said if we would just use our mustard seed of faith, we could move mountains.

What is your mountain? If you will trust God, He will move your mountain. Exercise your pure faith and believe God from your heart.

Most people can hardly believe I've had a stroke, because I seem so normal. Unless I tell them, they would never know that God has done such miraculous work in my life.

To the amazement of many, just a few months ago, I went to China. I was eighty-one and a half years old. It took 30 hours to get there and 30 hours to return. I never suffered jet lag going or coming home.

I want you to know that if you trust in the Lord and depend on Him, He has a work for you to do. As you endeavor to walk in obedience, He will certainly bring to pass the truth which He has spoken into your heart. In the word of God there is absolute truth. We can depend on Him, for He will bring it to pass, no matter how difficult it seems.

CHAPTER TWENTY-THREE

❧

Warring Against the Enemy

It was and still is exciting to follow the Lord on this supernatural walk of faith. God will take you places that you never dreamed you would go. Other times He will send you places that you don't necessarily want to go. He will have you do things you would rather avoid. But I've found that obedience is the best thing. I have proven it over and over. I must concede this supernatural walk of faith with the Lord has many times produced great pressure, sorrows and difficulties. But the Lord has always been faithful.

We have stood on the scripture in Isaiah 54:17, which reads, "No weapon that is formed against thee shall prosper; and every tongue that shall rise against thee in judgment thou shall condemn. This is the heritage of the servants of the Lord, and their righteousness is of me, saith the Lord."

Betty and I have stood on God's promises and kept trusting Him against every opposing force. We do wrestle against principalities and powers and spiritual wickedness in high places. It is not against flesh and blood, because we realize who our enemy is. Praise God, we have victory over all the power of the enemy.

I remember warring against the enemy, who was coming after our children. Our girls were brought up in the church. They taught Sunday school, sang solos, duets and trios with their mother, sang in the choir, starred in all the Christmas plays and were leaders in their youth groups. They loved the Lord, but when we sent them off to Christian college, we saw the enemy immediately putting in a bid for their souls.

We continued persevering to do the impossible, despite the devil's plan. Prior to leaving for college, our youngest daughter, Cyndi, had to be hospitalized on two occasions. Thinking her problem was solved on the first visit, they dismissed her. However, violent diarrhea and vomiting resumed almost as soon as we reached home. She had to be hospitalized again. It had been over a week since she had retained liquids or food in any form.

At the hospital, Cyndi was given fluids again and we were told she would be fine. She was released a second time, and again all the symptoms recurred. We knew she was very seriously dehydrated, but we had no diagnosis and no solution to cure her. As I prayed for her I could see that these symptoms were ravaging Cyndi's body and she had no relief or rest.

Desperate to help her, we cried out for help from above and the Lord began to reveal to me the fact that this was a demonic attack. I had to rise up against it and defeat the attacker. That whole evening and all through the night, I stood over her bed rebuking this enemy attack in the name of Jesus, telling the devil he could not have her.

I spoke blessing, healing and wholeness into her body in the name of Jesus. After days and nights of caring for Cyndi, Betty fell into a deep sleep as I continued the spiritual warfare. When she awoke and came to check Cyndi's condition, Betty saw the improvement instantly.

Cyndi said, "I'm feeling good! I'm feeling fine and I want something to eat!"

She began naming kinds of food she wanted eat and her mother said, "Oh no, you've got to stay on a liquid diet first, and slowly progress to solids."

"Let her eat whatever she wants," I replied. "The Lord has healed her and this problem is gone in Jesus' name."

Cyndi started with a shrimp cocktail, then salad, grilled steak and all the sides! God had delivered and healed her from this satanic attack.

That summer, when Cyndi was out of school, the Lord spoke to me again, saying the devil was going to try to kill her. Cyndi wasn't ardently following the Lord at this time. We had just helped her buy a new car just a few days prior. We usually joined hands, prayed and blessed her each day before she went to work. This particular morning, I gently told her what I had heard the Lord say to me. "Cyndi the devil has a desire to sift you like wheat," I explained.

I reminded her that Jesus told this to Peter on one occasion and we quickly discussed this passage. "Cyndi, I have prayed for you and everything is going to be OK. You are going to be alright." I didn't want to refer to the coming accident the Lord had already showed me.

One week later she called sobbing, "Dad! Dad, I've had a horrible accident. A truck hit me and spun the car around. And my car, you won't believe it, because it just looks like a total loss."

"But you're OK, aren't you?" I immediately asked.

Cyndi explained that she was a little shaken up, but she was all right. I told her that was all that really mattered and that I would be there right away. Her car was within $70 of being totaled. The insurance company decided to fix it instead of replacing it. God kept her safe, even though the car had spun around several times and landed in a service station's drive. God protected her and the devil lost; his plan was totally defeated.

Another time the devil tried to kill both my daughters. Sandi, our oldest, was living in Costa Mesa. Cyndi was visiting her so they could spend some time together. As sisters, they loved one another, loved to be together and were always great friends. Cyndi called me that evening to let me know that Sandi wanted her to spend the night.

Just that afternoon, the Lord had shown me that Sandi was going to have a very serious accident in her car and the devil planned to kill her sometime before the morning. I knew that she was going to total her car. I didn't reveal this to Cyndi, however. I told her she had to come home immediately. I told her I would explain in the morning.

Early the next morning, we received a call from Sandi. She had just been involved in an accident. Someone hit her, spun the car around several times and totaled her car. She said it was very frightening to her and the other passengers. She had some bruises, but the other passengers did not appear to be injured in any way. God had protected her and all those who were with her.

During my intercessory prayer time in my bedroom that day, I felt I was wrestling with a being I knew to be a demonic force. I continued to wrestle for some time, and then overpowered and sat on this demonic being, putting my hands around its neck.

With all authority that was granted me from the Lord I said, "In the name of Jesus, you cannot have my daughter Sandi. You take your filthy hands off her. The blood of Jesus Christ protects and covers her and she is protected and surrounded by angelic beings."

I then felt the release and I knew the victory was won. Almost immediately, my youngest daughter called. After the accident, I was able to tell both of them how God had protected them.

Many incidents occurred before Cyndi really totally surrendered her life to the Lord. On one occasion we were returning from a meeting in central California. Since she and her husband lived just a few miles off the freeway, we stopped for a visit. I was aware that neither of them was fervently following the Lord or interested in doing His will.

We were there on a Monday, and the Lord began telling me that my son-in-law Danny was going to be involved in a serious accident. I began to pray immediately and I was greatly troubled and burdened. I shared this with Betty and we both began to intercede.

The following Sunday evening we received a devastating call when we arrived home from church, for Cyndi had been frantically trying to get in touch with us. We had no answering machine, pager or cell phone in those days.

"Oh Dad," she cried. "I have been trying to reach you to tell you Danny's been in a terrible accident. He was riding his dirt bike out in the hills of Riverside. He is in a coma and they don't know if he will live."

"Cyndi," I said, "let me hang up so we can pray and ask God exactly what is to happen and what we are to do about this."

After prayer, I called and told her we were coming to the hospital. "Danny will live and not die, for God says His hand is upon him and He has this whole situation under control."

She was relieved that God was in control and that we were on our way to the hospital, which was over 100 miles away. When we arrived, Danny's family was distraught and suggested we should all pray that he would die, because the doctors were telling them if he lived he would be a vegetable.

"No," I replied. "God says he will not die and that He has His hands on him and this whole situation. God told me Danny would be restored and He would do a new thing in his life."

They weren't too happy with what I was saying, but I asked to go in privately and see him. I didn't want anyone coming in with me to hinder what God was telling me.

In his room, I said to Danny, "I know you can hear me even though you can't respond. I want you to know the Lord says you will live and not die and He will restore you."

I laid hands on him, saying, "I speak to your spirit. You shall live and you shall not die." He began to move a little bit, even though the doctors said he was in a deep coma.

This accident happened over 70 miles from where they lived, so we rented a hotel room for Cyndi, since she had no money and Danny had not been working for some time. She was expecting their first child and was over eight months pregnant. Betty and I worked to build her up, minister to her and help her in any way possible. The next day, when we went out to eat, I spoke to her about getting her soul right with the Lord.

"Dad," she said, "I don't smoke, drink or desire any of that. I have just wanted to run my own life."

I told her she had to let Jesus be Lord and also had to be strong for Danny. I told her we were going home and we were taking her car, because it would hardly run and needed a lot of work. I also told her we had friends in San Diego who had a motor home, so were going to contact them and ask if we could use it so she could stay on the hospital grounds.

Our precious friends gladly loaned us the motor home and, in a couple of days, we drove it up to Riverside. Cyndi lived in this motor home for nearly a month while Danny was in the coma. She totally surrendered her life to the Lord and we encouraged her to go everyday as much as they would allow and speak life into Danny, telling him that he would live and not die. The hospital personnel recognized she was going to be invaluable to his recovery and gave her complete access to be with Danny every day for as many hours as she wanted. Carrying her Bible with her, she would pray and speak healing into his spirit and body.

By this time, Cyndi was past due. So the doctors advised her to transfer her records and give birth to her baby in this hospital. She continued to grow stronger, spiritually speaking into Danny's life. Even though there were several critical times when they almost lost him, we all kept speaking life into him. After several weeks, Danny showed very positive signs of coming out of the coma. Slowly, he began to recognize us.

And then, suddenly, the hospital decided to transfer Danny to a Long Beach hospital where he could get further treatment and rehabilitation. This created a crisis for Cyndi, leaving her to give birth to the baby in Riverside when Danny was 75 miles away. Some of the staff realized her predicament, so they diligently tried to locate a hospital in Long Beach that would accept her. It seemed they were all refusing to take the responsibility, since the baby was past due. We kept praying and they finally persuaded St. Mary's in Long Beach to accept her. The hospital made one stipulation: she must come immediately for extensive exams, since she was so close to giving birth.

While Cyndi was being examined at St. Mary's Hospital, Betty and I drove up from San Diego in the motor home, bringing a baby bed and chest that we had purchased. Some of the procedures Cyndi experienced that day must have triggered her labor. As we were all trying to sleep together in the only bed across the back of the motor home, her labor pains began to progress. At 4 a.m., we decided it was time to leave for the hospital. Since our only transportation was the motor home, I jumped in the driver's seat so we could be quickly on our way.

Of course the motor home refused to start, even after several attempts. We all began praying and I commanded the vehicle to start in the name of Jesus. Thank the Lord, it started right up and we were off to the hospital.

I had been taking Lamaze classes to fill in for Danny, because Cyndi was determined to have a natural childbirth. After several hours in the labor room, the baby was born. What a glorious moment to be present when little Matt entered this world! Tears were running down both our faces. What a miracle! What a beautiful baby! He was very alert, with bright eyes open to see his new world.

God blessed us and provided even when it looked like there was no way. We would never, never have chosen for all these unfortunate events to happen in our youngest daughter's life. She didn't even have an opportunity to meet the doctor who would deliver her first son. But God worked all those difficult and nerve-wracking circumstances for good. We saw Cyndi's undisciplined lifestyle change. She became a mature, spiritually connected wife and mother who seemed far beyond her years in wisdom and experience. God was surely in control.

By the time the baby arrived, Danny was coming out of the coma. So he was able to learn that he had become a new father. Soon after, Danny surrendered his life to the Lord and he is walking with Lord to this day.

During his tough rehabilitation years, the state wanted to place him in training for janitorial work. But he had always had a wonderful mind for math. And since that ability remained, he insisted on pursuing training in the bio-medical field that was relatively new at that time. His goal was to repair the machines that helped keep him alive. Each time he was tested for a class he passed with brilliant grades.

The instructors tried to discourage him. They tried to place him in a menial job that would have cost them considerably less. But he was consistently at the top of his class, so they let him remain in the program. After three years he received a degree. Since his brain was severely damaged, this is a miracle of God for which he has always been grateful.

I want to encourage you to take hold of the promises of God. Believe God and believe His word as it says in Jeremiah 3:1, "Refrain thy voice from weeping and thine eyes from tears, for thy work shall be rewarded, saith the Lord, and they shall come again from the land of the enemy. There is hope in thine end, saith the Lord, that thy children shall come again to their own border. They will come from the land of the enemy."

My wife stood on this scripture for years and years and continues to stand on it today, for God is faithful to His word. Believe God that He will not only save you, but your whole household. Claim the promises, move in your mustard seed faith and hold God to His word. You may have to stand believing for some time and persevere with patience if it doesn't happen instantly.

Our oldest daughter has struggled most of her adult life, but we are still praying, speaking and believing God's Word until she is totally restored and walking consistently with the Lord. Her husband has never accepted or had interest in the things pertaining to God.

We believe that all changes in the name of Jesus, and our faith is steadfast and unmovable. Our daughter Sandra will be fervently on fire for God and will follow Him ardently. And we believe this in Jesus' name. Trust Him for your family and don't give up, because God is faithful to perform His word that He has spoken.

We send the word of God to your family, your children, your husband or wife, and will believe with you that God will deal with them. We ask Him to give them dreams in the nighttime, exposing them to the love, the power and the blessings of God. We speak this for your family in Jesus' name.

Chapter Twenty-Four

The Prophetic Word

We know there is great power in the prophetic word. God began using me in this gift in the early 1950s. At specific times, God has moved in my spirit and I have spoken under His anointing. As a result, I've seen many phenomenal things that He has done. Likewise, I believe many things I have spoken under the same anointing have happened, though I have not been present to see all the results.

When I think on the prophetic in God's Word, I am reminded of Ezekiel and the valley of the great dry bones that came alive when he spoke prophetically. There are many prophecies that are still to be fulfilled. **God's book** is full of the prophetic. As you study you will see in the Old Testament how the prophetic was spoken and then fulfilled in the New Testament.

Today, we see God with our own eyes, fulfilling the prophecies that were spoken thousands of years ago. **There is power in the prophetic and it will happen, if God said it through his true prophets.**

In the early '80s, I remember prophesying over a fellow minister who was in a wheelchair. His life was slipping away to bone cancer. We were attending a convention in Phoenix, and God called me to prophesy to the convention that God was going to heal his body. If I called him by name, many of you would remember him, for he was a famous, renowned minister that God used in this country and overseas.

When the Lord spoke the prophetic through me, I declared God would heal him, even though part of his spine had decayed from the cancer, and he would rise up from the wheelchair to preach the Word of God. It wasn't too many months later that he appeared on a television show, giving his testimony and relating the account of his tremendous miracle.

He had been in a meeting and was under a heavy anointing, preaching from his wheelchair. Under the inspiration of the Holy Spirit he began to quote, "The same Spirit that raised Christ from the dead, dwells in you," when he jumped out of the wheelchair and continued to preach the gospel! He was running all over the platform and his wife was so stunned and distressed, she ran to him and told him he must get back in the wheelchair. He hilariously gave the glory to the Lord and kept right on preaching as the audience could hardly restrain themselves.

Many times women or couples who could not have children would come to me or I would call them out in a service. I distinctly remember calling a certain couple forward during one service. I had never seen them before but as I was ministering to them I was impressed to ask them if they wanted to have a child. They said, "Yes, but we have been told we can not have children."

I prophesied and said that within a year she would bear a child. God opened her womb and within a year she had a child. I returned to minister there about a year later and they brought me the baby who had come forth by prophecy. I returned each year for the following three years and they brought another baby every year! God accomplished what the doctors said couldn't happen. I want you to know, when God speaks, it will happen if we walk in obedience and cooperate with Him.

On one occasion, while ministering in Mississippi, I called out a woman for whom the Lord had given me a word of encouragement. In addition, the Lord said that she was going to have a baby.

"Oh no," she exclaimed, "I don't want any more children."

"But you are going to have one," I countered.

When I returned a year later, the mother came bringing the child those prophetic words had said she would have. She told me this precious little boy, who was considerably younger than her other children, had already been the greatest blessing to the family. Her husband was away in medical school and this beloved new child was filling every minute of their time with great joy and comfort.

Still, she kept her distance from me saying, "Don't prophecy over me again. I definitely do not want any **more** children!"

One of my best friends in the San Diego area had only one daughter. At 60 years old, he wanted grandchildren. So he brought his daughter and son-in-law to the church where I was pastoring. After the service they told me of their desperation, for she had not been able to conceive. As I began to pray, the Lord moved in my spirit and I began to prophesy that she would soon conceive and they would have a boy and he would be called into the ministry.

They went away rejoicing and praising God. In just a few months, she conceived and they had a beautiful boy and my friend had a grandson – a child who has brought the most unbelievable joy and happiness to his life.

A couple of years ago, my friend's daughter called and told me her son was being ordained into the ministry. She invited me to be a part of that meaningful occasion but, since I was thousands of miles away, I was not able to attend. God gave them the desire of their hearts and He is faithful as we continue to trust in Him, to accomplish what seems impossible to man.

Many times God gives prophetic words that are corrective and directive. According to the Word of God, a prophecy that is given through the gift of prophecy is given simply for edification, exhortation and comfort. Corinthians, chapter 12 tells us this gift of prophecy is not given for correction and direction.

God uses the second ministry gift, as recorded in Ephesians 4:11 to speak forth a word of correction or future direction. **I want you to know that if you will believe God's Word in faith and speak prophetic** words of edification, exhortation and comfort over your children, your family or any circumstances you face can change according to God's word. Find a word in scripture that you can stand on, believe it and keep speaking it. Because God will accomplish it, for He is faithful to perform His word and to bring it to pass.

CHAPTER TWENTY-FIVE

❧

A Trip to China

During September and October of 2009, God sent me to China. I was almost 81 years old, but God's strength, blessing and anointing was strongly upon me. I traveled for about 30 hours to get there. I went from Denver to Los Angeles, Los Angeles to Shanghai and Shanghai to Chongqing, which is a city of 35 million.

I arrived in the morning and was scheduled for a meeting that evening in an underground church. We had to be very careful that the police didn't find our location. I stayed in a beautiful hotel and was registered under another name. It was one of the most beautiful, unique hotels I've ever seen.

During the first meeting, God showed His power through tremendous signs and wonders. It was exciting to see the hunger and the desire the Chinese people have for God. Friends of mine who ministered in China in the 1940s were driven out when the bamboo curtain came down in 1949. All the missionaries had to leave the country, but they boldly proclaimed the church would go underground and persevere, despite the persecution.

How right on they were, for I encountered strong, devoted and committed Christians. Thanks be to God for these faithful missionaries who followed the call to that nation, withstood the tests and gave up their comforts. Some even gave their lives or the lives of their children. They paved the way and what a reward they will receive!

While I was in China, meetings were held at different times and places to avoid discovery by the government. In all meetings, the response to ministry was overwhelming, for God would bless, heal and baptize the people in the Holy Spirit.

I worked hard to show how God desired to use them in greater ways in the power of the Spirit. I knew I would be there for only a short time and I could sense a great need in their lives for the Spirit's empowerment. I taught them that they were God's messengers and His voices and must be full of the Holy Spirit and power. In every meeting, I asked those who wanted to receive the baptism of the Holy Spirit, speaking with other tongues, to come forward. Many would respond and I taught them how to receive the Spirit.

After prayer with them, I commanded them to receive and they immediately began speaking in their heavenly language. I encouraged them to speak for 10 minutes or more because I wanted to make sure they received a good dose of the Holy Ghost. They were very loud and extremely blessed. They were so elated when they saw the power of God in action and the gifts of the Spirit flowing during our ministry. I felt it was pivotal to teach them that the Lord had the same power and gifts available for them to heal the sick; see miracles, signs and wonders; and cast out demons in the name of Jesus. God began doing great and wonderful things as they began to grab hold of this truth. He began working through them in healing and in casting out evil spirits.

Some were saved, but there weren't many sinners in attendance since they had to be extremely careful about whom they invited to the underground church in order to prevent those who had evil intentions from infiltrating their meetings.

At one meeting, 30 were baptized in the Holy Spirit, spoke in other tongues and endued with the power of God. I let them know that speaking in tongues and having a prayer language was the invaluable evidence, but the primary achievement in receiving the baptism was being filled with the mighty power of God. Scripture says that when you are filled with the power of God, or dynamite from the Greek translation, you are empowered by His spirit and enabled to do great things in the name of the Lord.

Jesus says, "I give you the keys of the kingdom of heaven and whatever you bind here on earth will be bound in heaven, and whatever you loose on earth shall be loosed in heaven." The keys speak of authority and, before Jesus ascended to heaven, He told the disciples He would send the Comforter and they would receive power after the Holy Ghost had come upon them and they would be His witnesses. This promise is also for the **now**!

I taught the Chinese people that when the power of the Spirit comes upon us, we receive power to do wonders, signs and miracles as the body of Christ. They received this glorious experience so exuberantly and I just allowed them to absolutely dive in with every ounce of energy. It was exciting to see their desperation in seeking, knowing and believing God, for they truly wanted to be full of the Holy Spirit.

To my knowledge, everyone who came to every service was filled with the Holy Spirit, speaking with other tongues. There was only one little girl, maybe three years of age, that I questioned. But all the others signified they had received the Holy Spirit, speaking with other tongues. One woman was spinning around like a top, her hands in the air and her eyes closed as she spoke in another language, giving glory and praise to God. Many testified of healings occurring in their bodies as they were being baptized in the fire of the Holy Spirit. God did wonderful, magnificent and marvelous things in all of the services.

Nearly all the services were four hours in length, but as far as the people were concerned, the meetings didn't ever need to end! There was such hunger and they sang with such joy and enthusiasm and the time flew by. I loved what God was doing in China! They tell me there are one hundred to one hundred and fifty million dedicated Christians in China, not just professing, but those who are devoted to the Lord Jesus Christ and have sold out to Him.

I held many services all over Chongqing. We rode public transportation and walked a lot. Chonqing is a city of nearly 35 million people – that's almost the population of the state of California. Each time we left the hotel we moved among the multitudes. The people live in high-rise apartments and I have never seen so many never-ending, skyscrapers.

What a blessing it was to minister to the precious people in Chongqing. Thank God for opening this door for me at my age and imparting to me supernatural energy and strength. I began to realize God was granting me energy during the very first meeting, for I was not able to sleep or cat nap during the flights to China. It was as if Satan arranged disturbing set-ups: the unending crying of a baby across from me and constant loud talking behind me, etc. Yet, here I was, ministering with no jet lag and with my body refreshed and invigorated. Unmistakably, God's anointing and blessings rested on me constantly during my ministry in China, because my schedule required many hours each day.

I also ministered in Chendu, a smaller city of 10 million. We ministered for a three-day weekend, conducting three services each day, primarily ministering and teaching church leadership. After each four-hour session they would bring me a sandwich or some type of food before resuming the next session. It was three very long, but significantly fruitful days. The Lord allowed me to impart His power, His anointing and gifts of the Spirit to those precious leaders.

I will not forget one of the last prophetic words which the Lord spoke through me. It was a difficult one for me to deliver, as the Lord told them they were being prepared for a season of greater persecution that was coming to China's true Christians.

Recently, Betty and I became aware that much time had passed since we had received a newsletter or heard from our precious missionary hosts of the China ministry. We phoned their mother who told us that my last prophetic word was already happening. They are now forced to be extremely careful: no mail, emails or phone calls, for the enemy is watching and listening. Pray for the safety of these precious people. Even as the enemy's plan accelerates, the Spirit of God will raise up a standard against him. What a comfort to know unequivocally that no government, no power can ever stop this end time move of God or the gospel being preached in every nation, tribe and tongue! Praise His holy name!

CHAPTER TWENTY-SIX

❦

Admonition

I want you to know the best is yet to come. God is going to do greater things than we can even imagine. We must allow ourselves to be open to Him and to the moving of the gifts of the Spirit. We must let these gifts of the Spirit flow out of us every place we go, so we may meet the needs of the people. Let the Lord lead you in the marketplace, when you are putting gas in your car, in restaurants, in hardware stores and grocery stores. When He gives you compassion for someone, be bold, be the hands, feet, eyes and ears of the Lord and speak life into that person. God is going to use you in a great way. Prepare yourself for the greatest move of the Spirit the church has ever seen!

Many people refer to the ministries of Smith Wigglesworth, Aimee Semple McPherson and Maria Woodworth Etter, for they were all used mightily in the power of the Spirit. Perhaps you may not have heard of Sister Etter, but she had a great and powerful ministry, starting in the 1880s and over two decades in the early twentieth century.

Her granddaughter attended our church in Indianapolis and she told us about many of the wonderful miracles that happened during her lifetime. We were able to get Sister Etter's diary that tells of many astounding signs and wonders during her ministry.

Once, as Sister Etter was preaching in a church in Indianapolis, she suddenly froze with her right hand in the air and her mouth open. She stood in that position for 24 hours. She never moved a muscle and never batted an eye. We were told that police came, doctors came and many others came to see this phenomenon but it didn't phase her. She continued standing there, not moving a muscle, as she was under the power of God. After the 24-hour period, she came out of the trance and went on preaching where she left off, never knowing what had happened. For up to 20 miles around where she was holding services, men and women were struck down in homes, in businesses, on roads and in streets under the power of God. Some lay for hours and had wonderful visions.

I want to tell you that these great anointings will manifest again soon and similar miracles will happen. The Lord still has all these types of anointing and He is getting the body of Christ ready to pour them out once more. He is going to use the body, for there are not enough ministers, apostles, prophets, evangelists, pastors and teachers for Him to use in these last days to do all His phenomenal work. He is preparing all of us and will send the body of Christ forward to do great signs and wonders.

In Corinthians 12 you can read about the gifts which are for the body of Christ, not just for the preachers, apostles, prophets, evangelists, pastors and teachers who are the five-fold ministry. When the Holy Spirit is released within the prepared body of Christ, out of their belly shall flow rivers of living water. In this river, that represents the Holy Spirit, there will be every provision that is needed, allowing the gifts of the Spirit to work through those who will believe and go forth.

God is preparing you. If you are going through difficulties and problems you don't understand, just know that God is preparing you for a greater ministry. He is getting you ready so that you will be strong and have iron in your soul as you go forth into this world of wickedness. You will not crumble under the opposition that the enemy will bring. You will overcome the enemy. Signs and wonders and miracles and healings will transpire.

The gifts of healing, faith, miracles, prophetic utterances, words of knowledge, words of wisdom and discerning of spirits, tongues and interpretation of tongues are all given to the body to equip them as they go forth, operating with this powerful anointing. And the world will marvel and will wonder what is going on.

I say to you, "Just be ready and be available to the Lord. Don't think it strange concerning the fiery trial that is trying you. God is preparing you for a great work. Remember, the greater the building that is to be erected, the deeper the foundation must be. God is building the foundation so that you might be strong and do mighty exploits in His name."

The Lord wants me to encourage you to walk by faith and not by sight. Step out of the boat and believe God for the impossible. God is calling the church out to walk in the supernatural as He called Peter out of the boat. You, too, can walk on water in the supernatural as you rely on the Lord and trust in Him. He has everything well in hand even though the world is a mess and full of trepidation and anxiety.

There are great storms coming, but the Lord is in control and nothing can happen that He doesn't allow. This will be the greatest opportunity for the church to move forward, believing God for the signs, the wonders and the miracles. This will be a great move of the Spirit of God doing the works of Jesus.

It says in Mark 11, "Whosoever will say unto this mountain be thou removed and be thou cast into the sea and shall not doubt in his heart but shall believe that those things which he saith shall come to pass, he shall have whatsoever he saith."

Declare now that you will receive all these great anointings that God gave to His great men and women thousands of years ago. We have seen God give little tidbits of what is to come. Therefore, be available, be disciplined, be prepared and declare you will be part of this great end-time army that is about to be turned loose. Be sure that you are available! Make this your prayer: "Here I am Lord, I want to be what you want me to be and I am available. Anoint and use me to be part of your army. Let the gifts of the Spirit flow through me."

I feel the Spirit speaking that we should all fast and pray, crying out and seeking the Lord with all our hearts. Get your Bible and open it to

I Corinthians chapters 12 and 14. Study until you are convinced these gifts are not just for some special, super saints the Lord favors, but are to operate through you as a believer. Then on your knees ask the Lord what gifts He wants to use through you."

Say, "Here I am Lord. Like Isaiah of old, send me."

You will not necessarily quit your jobs, but you will go to the marketplace, to your jobs and to all those to whom you make contact and God will use you powerfully."

Also, read I Corinthians chapter 13, for we need to be filled with God's love. The scripture teaches us the gifts of the Spirit and faith work by love. If you are filled with love, the gifts will have greater potency and power for those to whom you minister. Let the anointing of the Holy Spirit come into you and then flow out of you. Read Galatians chapter 5 about the fruit of the Spirit. We need the fruit of the Spirit if the gifts of the Spirit are going to flow out of us and be effective in our lives. The gifts of the Spirit are given to us, but the fruit of the Spirit is produced from the way we live our lives. God wants to instill fruit in our lives, so search your heart; do some fasting, praying and believing that God will work through you.

CHAPTER TWENTY-SEVEN

❧

Betty's Perspective – From the Beginning

My life began on April 28, 1932, in a humble farmhouse in Pleasantville, Indiana, in Sullivan County. The house belonged to my maternal grandparents, Herbert and Ellen Jackson. I was the first and only daughter born to proud parents Cecil Jacob and Mary Lorraine Enochs.

My father was the seventh son of Charles Wesley and Mary Adams Enochs. He was always proud of his name's Biblical roots and similarities: Enoch was the seventh child from Adam, my father's mother's name was Adams, and he was a seventh son.

When my father was two years old, his mother died during childbirth along with the new sister, Iris, leaving his father with one older daughter and seven sons. His older sister took the place of his mother until his father found a wonderful Pentecostal Church of God widow to become his wife. She had two children, and they had one daughter together.

My grandfather became one of the early Pentecostal preachers, ministering in the brush arbors across southern Indiana. This was not long after the Azusa Street outpouring and these Spirit-filled preachers and layman endured much persecution. They were recipients of much ridicule and sometimes the targets of rotten eggs. But appropriate honor should be theirs, for they paved the way for the spirit-filled church today.

My Daddy was raised in the church and I heard him tell about the **Glory Plus** services for the adults which were filled with miracles, healings, hilarious shouting and powerful singing, and it seemed heaven was coming to earth. However, they offered no teaching or ministry to the children and young people. Since the outpouring was so new, many felt if men attempted to organize in any way, it might give place to the divisiveness of the enemy and they would go the way of all the other denominations.

Daddy recalled playing outside the church while his mom and dad had a shouting, glorious time inside. He also shared that, even though he had rebelled against God, in his father's home he could not get away from the amazing power of the Holy Spirit's call upon his life. He knew he must also preach the gospel.

My maternal great-grandparents, Elmer and Mary Jackson, were faithful Methodists and my mother attended Sunday school with them as a child. She was pianist for their church during her early teen years. Her parents were good, moral people, but never attended God's house. She was the oldest of four girls, and a brother was added to the family some years later.

Mother and father lived on neighboring farms and attended the same small high school. Teen love led to early marriage. Since coal mining and farming were the only two vocational choices, my folks moved to New Castle, Indiana, when I was two years old. My Dad was hired at the Chrysler factory. During this time, my father spent a lot of time with a pretty rough crowd, leaving my mother home to tend little Betty.

One weekend when they were visiting back home, Mother gave Daddy an ultimatum. That weekend, my grandfather called and strongly urged my parents to attend a service where he was preaching that evening. When the salvation invitation was given, my Dad went forward and a woman came to Mother, telling her she should also join her husband so they could be a Christian family. The woman stayed with me and Mother went forward, making a decision to serve the Lord and to go back to New Castle. My parents immediately found a good Full Gospel church where they endeavored to be devoted followers and faithful leaders in the work of the Lord.

Watching the power of the Holy Spirit and the many miracles at church made an indelible impression on me during my early childhood. In a mission where my parents ministered, I vividly remember a woman who had been blind from birth, and I witnessed the emotional response she had when she saw for the first time in her life.

When my brother was about two years old, he fell under the tire of our car as it rolled backwards. His leg was smashed completely flat. I still recall the graphic picture of tire marks on one side of his leg, and gravel on the other. My father stood him up, but his leg collapsed and he could not stand. We were ready to leave for Sunday morning services, so my parents prayed and my brother screamed as we made the trip. As all the people of God surrounded him, powerfully entreating the Lord for his healing, I saw his leg expand and become normal. His screaming ceased and when they stood him on his feet, he began running around the church. My brother had no symptoms or lasting effects stemming from the accident.

These are only two of the numerous miracles that made a lasting impression on my life. During those years we had extremely long services every night with one revival after another. I have no doubt that we lived in a realm of the supernatural, for I never remember lack of sleep hindering me from getting to school on time or lack of time for homework affecting my grades.

In my early teen years, my father accepted the pastorate of a church in Alfordsville, Indiana. Alfordsville was a very small town, surrounded by a farming community. The church and parsonage were around two and a half miles from the town. By then I had two brothers, Jerry who was four years younger, and Paul who was born when I was 12. The community was blessed with an abundance of boys in the church and on nearby farms. However, there were no girls even near my age. So I found intense delight in reading and studying and had an overwhelming desire to sing and play the piano.

Each day after chores I would go to the church in an attempt to get better on the piano. Mother taught me the musical scales and gave me a few piano lessons with a woman who taught me to chord with my left hand.

One day my dad informed me that I was going to accompany him as he sang at the high school Baccalaureate service. He gave me his choice of song and music, but I protested. I told him I couldn't play in public. He laid his hand on the top of my head and said, "Oh yes, you will play in public, and it will be beautiful."

Reflecting back, it was at that moment that I began playing in octaves, finding new chords and making chord runs. My playing was a gift from God that enabled me to play in countless services and in some unbelievable places during my life. Reading musical scores seemed unnecessary for me since the talent came from within. But when I began leading choirs and writing music, I wanted to improve my skill for reading music. When we pastored in Saginaw, there were college music majors in my choir, but the Lord anointed and enabled me.

In late summer of 1948, my father was called to pastor a church in Kokomo, Indiana, just 50 miles north of Indianapolis. I felt disappointed that I wouldn't be able to graduate with my class of 20 students, especially since I had the highest grade-point average. But my desire had always been to please the Lord and my parents. So I realized, if my father and mother knew this to be the will of God for them, then how could I be sad?

School in Kokomo was a challenge. The classes were so different from my former small school which offered minimum classes. With the Lord's help, I made it through my junior year. I worked hard to meet the challenges of my senior year and get sufficient credits for graduation.

Socially, I was delighted to have so many girls waiting to be my friends. I found some that really desired to please the Lord. The teenage years were difficult for many. Worldly pleasures, which were considered sinful then, were successfully used by the devil to pull children away from the Lord and the church. But my overwhelming desire to please the Lord and find His will for my life was pivotal. I had no desire to partake of anything that would displease the Lord.

I had been aware of the Lord's call since I was 12 years old. It was secretly, but utmost in my heart. The vision I had received remained hidden in my heart, but I knew without a doubt that I must marry the right man for this vision to be materialized.

It seemed inconceivable at this time not to have a steady boyfriend. But my parents squashed any ideas of dating alone. They were not going to allow their daughter to repeat their own mistakes and relive the struggles of teen marriage. So my boyfriend and I went on group dates to permissible places with early curfews. My mother was not pleased with my choice of boyfriend, because she doubted his sincerity with the Lord. He went to considerable lengths to pursue me and, as time passed, he caused me constant aggravation.

His behavior and conduct were exactly the opposite of what my mother expected. Meanwhile, I rolled along, very disillusioned with what I thought was love. Of course later I realized I had not the slightest concept of real love, nor what to look for in a lifelong mate.

Eventually I started to notice a handsome young man who appeared in the church orchestra playing a beautiful Gibson electric guitar. Asking around among my friends, I learned he came from a Bible college in Minneapolis with the brother of a friend of mine. He was looking for work in our area.

Each time we played, he waited for me to sign or mouth the key for that particular song. Back in those days there were no prerequisites and no practices for the orchestra and it was glorious just to have more people use their talent for the Lord.

Those were the days when we played and sang with great anticipation for the Holy Spirit to take over the service in a powerful way. It was not unusual for 15 people to simultaneously hit the floor and begin dancing before the Lord. Not one of them encountered obstacles or hindrances, but with joy they glorified the Lord. We felt this was a clear-cut experience of dancing in the Spirit. It was at a later time in my life when I found the word of God in Psalms, commanding us all to dance before the Lord in praise and thanksgiving. I took intense delight in this experience and found it to be vital in my life.

Somewhere around the first of November 1949, the handsome young man asked if he could take me home from church on Sunday evening. From our first date, there was no doubt in my mind that Howard's call to the ministry was foremost in his life. From our conversations, I observed that pastoring was his primarily focus. Living in a pastor's home for years had prepared me for Howard's calling and consequently it was easy to merge the clarity of our visions. It was with much anticipation and intense delight that I become a pastor's wife at 19 years of age.

Chapter Twenty-Eight

Betty's Perspective — Coherence Achieved

The sacrifices ahead seemed insignificant even though we both left what were considered great-paying jobs back then. We had no children to cloth or feed and the Lord gave me the ability to plan our meals on a low budget. I found a friend whose husband took old sewing machines and electrified them, so I asked her if I could borrow one to make my first Easter dress. On my birthday, April 28, I received a card from those dear ones informing me that the sewing machine was their gift to me. This gift was so important in my life. Sewing was pretty much a necessity for two daughters and myself.

Later, sewing became joy and revealed another creative gift from God. Over the years, Howard provided the latest machines and sergers, plus a room of my very own. During our pastorates, retreating to this room and engaging in a sewing project provided me a therapeutic release from all the church conundrums. It was a release from the pressures and responsibilities of the ministry.

When we made the dedication to pioneer the first church in Gary, we claimed the wonderful promises of God to help us through the formidable and difficult places and make us effective. I recognized immediately that God had sent my husband there to not only build a congregation, but a church structure for the glory of God in that community. His compliance to that assignment from the Lord was such that he would have given his life if necessary. From the beginning of our ministry together I realized it was a great privilege to stand with this extremely obedient man of God. I grew into total agreement with him in God's plan for our lives.

I knew Howard heard from God and I had no doubt that the Holy Spirit spoke to him supernaturally. Through the years, I decided that it was not so necessary for me to hear God personally. Actually, I recognized it was safer for Howard to hear from the Lord. Then I would be less responsible for hearing incorrectly.

Looking back on my life, I find that God has endowed me with many talents on which I have relied. Howard has remarked many times how grateful he is that, since I was his pianist, he could always start services on time.

After the church building was complete we both wanted an organ. But since there were no funds in the church treasury available, we bought a Hammond Spinet in our name and signed a contract for $30 per month. It was delivered to the church on a Saturday afternoon. I had never played an organ, but Howard believed I would be playing that next morning. The foot keys and pedal were strange to me, but I acted on his faith and my knowledge of the keyboard and played like a pro on Sunday morning.

This was another supernatural talent from the Lord and, to this day, playing the organ is one of my true loves. As I trusted wholly and unreservedly in the Lord, He showed me that in His **grace** there was the divine ability to do what He called me to do. So I kept doing the tasks He set before me. The Lord helped me with writing and conducting programs for Christmas, Easter, Sunday school, women's ministry, children and youth, as well as with office skills to assist my husband.

As time passed, I must confess my soul sometimes became troubled and I questioned several of the assignments the Lord laid upon Howard. I could plainly see God used him to obliterate man-rule and establish the Biblical pattern of New Testament church leadership. But I just couldn't understand how, after all the inescapable and unavoidable conflicts we endured in order to finally establish the proper foundation for growth, we had to move on to another assignment - especially an assignment where I quickly found yet another challenge worse than the last.

Complaining became my portion, since I couldn't understand why we could not remain and see the fruits of our labors. I had no doubt that I shared my life with a man who was totally obedient to God's destiny for his life. I felt he suffered distress, anguish and rejection without reward. Consoling myself with the fact he had the great wisdom and God-given ability to hear the Lord's strategy for each situation, I steadily endeavored to use my talents to help him in other areas of the ministry.

Through the years, I learned God's plan for our lives always involved our gifts, His timing and our being in the right place at the right time. In addition, I found there were obstacles which could keep these three things from appearing – mainly fear of failure, not wanting to leave our comfort zone and being influenced by other people's points of view. Using my gifts was never a problem for me. But understanding God's timing and being in the right place at the right time proved extremely difficult.

When God arranged for us to be in Korea in 1973, new seeds were planted in our spirits which put us in direct alignment with God's destiny for our lives. When we were stirred in our spirits during daily prayer time one day, I sensed God was stirring our nest and just might be telling us to launch out of our comfort zones. As Howard began telling me of the visions God was giving him, I pictured the Lord opening another church which would be more passionate toward missions, so Howard could fulfill these pressing visions he was receiving. Consequently, I began to prepare myself for another extremely painful farewell, as once again we would be leaving the precious ones God had given us to shepherd.

Our oldest daughter, Sandi, was a beautiful girl with a voice like a heavenly angel. When Sandi was in her second year at a Christian college in Costa Mesa, California, our youngest daughter graduated early from high school and entered the same college.

I wasn't prepared for empty nest syndrome, but Cyndi had won a teen talent competition in the fall and earned a college scholarship. In college, Sandi was a soloist in an elite musical group. She had arranged an audition for Cyndi with the college music director. He was so impressed with her talent that he urged Cyndi to enroll as soon as possible. Cyndi had never been the studious one, but she immediately won the hearts and abundant favor of everyone she met. I knew her push for early graduation and her rush to college weren't based on academic achievement, but it seemed the Lord was working on her behalf.

The two beautiful, empty rooms at the top of the stairs were unbearably difficult for both Howard and me. The personal emotional pain I was suffering only intensified when I had a freak fall and broke my left foot. Now I was grounded on the first floor. I still recall my ridiculous pity parties, for I missed the assistance of the girls so much. Even loading the dishwasher was a new task for me. But it was all in the plan of almighty God, for now I could not busy myself during this time of loneliness and uncertainty about our future.

As I entered into hours of prayer and fasting with my husband, God began to open my spirit to a new spiritual dimension. I became aware of a new thing happening to Howard and I could sense a change in his spirit that I had never known before. Some of his traditional attitudes seemed to be fading away.

I began to entreat the Lord to show me the same visions He gave Howard. I struggled immensely when Howard began telling me that, in this new ministry, which would take us all over the world, we could not ask for a meeting or ask for money. This seemed utterly ridiculous to me. I had a great gift for public relations and, if we were being called into evangelism, I could call friends all over the county and get an itinerary ready in no time.

When I shared this with my husband, he replied, "No Betty, God will open the doors he has for ministry and He will supply the finances."

With all the radical changes my husband was experiencing, I began to wonder if he was in mid-life crisis.

Never before had I doubted what my husband was hearing from the Lord, so I began to earnestly ask the Lord to confirm the words to me so I could enthusiastically walk with him in the same path. Remember that I had not consistently and personally desired to hear God's voice, because I depended on my husband, since he heard so accurately.

As I steadily endeavored to support Howard's decisions, the Lord graciously sent His heroes in the faith to minister to me, personally confirming our future call together. For the first time in our ministry, God graciously gave me sisters in the Lord with whom I could actually share my personal anxieties – both about our call from the Lord and my concern over my daughter's deteriorating spiritual condition while attending Christian college.

I just don't have words to express the joy I felt in those new relationships. As a pastor's wife, I could not show partiality in the church. So I had no close relationships and most certainly could not share problems in my family.

During this time the Holy Spirit inspired me to write a Covenant between the Lord and us with passages from the Word of God. It covered several areas of our life, including our daughters. As I wrote, I made each scripture personal by adding their names:

Isaiah 54:13, "And Sandi and Cyndi shall be disciples, taught by you Lord and great shall be the peace and undisturbed composure of Sandi and Cyndi."

Jeremiah 31:16 and 17, "I will refrain my voice from weeping and my eyes from tears for my work shall be rewarded and Sandi and Cyndi shall return from the enemy's land and there is hope in my future, for Sandi and Cyndi shall come again to our land."

Isaiah 59:21, "Your covenant with me, Father is: My Spirit who is upon you and my words which I have put in your mouth (The Words of God my Father) shall not depart out of my mouth, or out of the mouths of Sandi and Cyndi or out of the mouths of my children's children says the Lord from henceforth and forever!"

This passage from Isaiah is a powerful scripture which has been fulfilled in Cyndi and her two sons, Matt and Josh. I have prayed these powerful words from the Word of God for 35 years.

Howard has already shared with you the outstanding and accurate prophetic words which confirmed God's call to this supernatural walk in 1975. Outstanding in my mind was the surprise meeting with Dr. J. Robert Ashcroft, formerly the president of Evangel College in Springfield, Missouri. (He was also the father of our late attorney general, John Ashcroft.)

Dr. Ashcroft was introduced as the full-time International Director of Ministry and Prayer for the FGBMFI when we first attended their international breakfast. We highly respected this general of God. Though we had never met him personally, we had sat under his powerful teaching numerous times. We were thrilled to be invited to lunch with him, for he said there was something extremely important he wanted to tell us. He related to us that the Lord had given him a word of knowledge for us.

"A new ministry is ahead for you and you must not have fear," he told us, "for it will be the greatest ministry of your life. The decisions you make in the near future are vital in the development of this future ministry."

Dr. Ashcroft proceeded to give us much encouragement about the decisions we had already made and assured us we were on the right road for the perfect plan of God.

He also gave us two scriptures which were vital for our futures:

Proverbs 16:7, "When man's ways please the Lord, He maketh even his enemies to be at peace with him."

And Isaiah 54:17, "No weapon formed against thee shall prosper, and every tongue that shall rise against thee in judgment, thou shalt condemn. This is the heritage of the servants of the Lord, and their righteousness is of me, saith the Lord."

Once more, being in the right place at the right time was significant, because we knew some of our peers already believed we were going off the deep end. During this reshaping period, we opened our hearts and readily accepted those whom God sent with words of encouragement, knowledge and prophecy for our lives. Over and over we learned crucial lessons about being in the right place at the right time when the Lord has called you to walk supernaturally in a life of faith.

When Howard accepted the invitation to minister with FGBMFI in Italy and Sicily in September 1975, he told me I should go with him. We would buy my round-trip ticket to Philadelphia where we would meet with the group to fly to Italy. He felt God wanted to teach me to walk supernaturally and, therefore, I needed to find the faith to believe for the round-trip fare from Philadelphia to Italy.

I began to talk to the Lord very carefully, as I realized I must begin to hear from Him for my individual needs. I had a chest full of material, so I made a new suitable traveling wardrobe, remembering God's plans always include using our gifts. I proclaimed to everyone I met that I was going but, as per usual, His timing never seems to occur at the same time as ours. I endeavored to use every particle of my mustard seed faith.

Three days before the money was due to arrive in Philadelphia, we attended the International breakfast meeting of the FGBMFI in Anaheim. There were others in attendance that morning who were going on the Italy trip, and the leaders invited all who were members of the team up for prayer. I went forward in faith, calling the things that were not as if they were.

As the leaders were laying hands on each of us, I felt a big, warm hand on my back. As sure as I knew my name was Betty, I heard the

Lord say, "I am speaking to this brother to pay your way to Italy and back."

I was ecstatic and could hardly wait to see it play out. After the meeting concluded, a precious woman whom I had just met the week before approached me. We had discussed our children, but neither Howard nor I had expressed my need with anyone.

She said to me, "I don't want to embarrass you with this question, but do you have your tickets to Italy?"

I answered no and she continued, "During prayer for the team, I felt God was saying we should pay your way, so I just spoke to my husband and he confirmed that the moment he laid his hand on your back, God said, "Pay her way to Italy.""

I rejoiced as she wrote me a check for the total amount needed, for this was one of the first miracles for me personally in this life of walking supernaturally.

Another of my struggles was the manner in which the Lord was changing Howard's ministry, for it seemed he could no longer preach sermons in the powerful, anointed way in which I was accustomed. He seemed destined only to share – telling what God was doing in our lives. People seemed to relate positively to his sharing and were extremely blessed. But I couldn't help asking, "Why can't he preach sermons anymore?"

My primary frustration came when he began to minister to individuals with definite, specific words. He would say things that he could not have known, for I knew he had never seen these people before. Those to whom he ministered were abundantly elated and blessed that the Lord would give individual knowledge and wisdom about their problems and circumstances. Again though, I couldn't help asking, "Oh my Lord, what if he is wrong?"

Through the years I knew my husband could see very vivid things about people which he could not have personally known or learned. When the things he shared with me would indisputably happen just as he said they would, I wondered how he could have possibly known in such detail. Looking back, I see how powerfully God used these gifts during the ministry assignments He gave us. As these gifts were becoming more dominant during our services, I was seeing their primary importance in the body of Christ and I began to covet these gifts working in my own life.

When we make ourselves available, wholly and unreservedly, the Lord will begin to identify areas of our lives where we need to observe His supernatural intervention. For several years I suffered with a large plantar wart on the ball of my right foot. I sought help from doctors and specialists who tried several methods to remove it, but to no avail. They said it needed to be surgically removed, but cutting nerves in that area could not be avoided and could end up making the situation worse.

My family was appalled when, once a month, I would take a razor blade and shave off a few layers so I could press the piano pedal or gas pedal of the car without so much pain. Before leaving for our trip to Italy, I developed 15 small warts around the area of my big toe. Believe me when I say prayer had been sought arduously for this infirmity.

During Howard's ministry in Sicily, He called out a healing as the Lord was telling Him someone had a growth on the bottom of his or her foot. The Holy Spirit was directing that person to act on this word, stamp his or her foot on the floor three times and the affliction would be healed.

During this time, I was playing the organ softly. I thought about this word, but dismissed it as being for the Sicilian people to whom we were ministering. Just then, Howard was directed to emphasize the same word and he repeated it exactly. Immediately I knew the word was for me and I took my foot from the expression pedal, stamped it to the floor three times and said, "Thank you Lord, I am healed!"

Knowing that I fussed with this foot so much, I felt the Lord saying, "I receive your thanks and you are healed, but you are not to look at your foot or even say a word about it until you get home."

We had about 10 days before returning home and it was difficult not to look at my foot! But it was joyous to have no more pain. When we arrived home, I could hardly wait to get into the tub for a good soak in a bubble bath. I jumped into the tub, grabbed my foot and saw the bottom of my foot looking just like a beautiful baby's skin. The large wart was gone, along with the 15 small ones!

I screamed at the top of my lungs and Howard came running, ready to fend off an attacker. Instead, he found me rejoicing over God's miracle healing which I received through Howard's obedience to allow the Holy Spirit's gifts to flow through him and my obedience to accept the Spirit's instruction.

This miracle was not only a blessing to me, but also a great testimony to my family and to all those knowing the years of pain I endured. God was teaching me more and more about our supernatural walk together and I knew from that experience that I could absolutely depend upon and trust Him to lead us just as he led the children of Israel when the Word said, "He took them by their hand and led them."

There remained, however, a nagging mystery in my mind, soul and spirit regarding the unprecedented manner of the ministry God had given Howard. As I reflected over our ministry assignments, I felt I needed clarity.

The Lord led me to write a dissertation on the New Testament fivefold governmental ministries of the church according to Ephesians 4:11 and 12. During this intensive study, the Lord revealed to me that most of the present body of Christ do not understand or put into operation the government He established in the early church, and which still remains His pattern for today.

He let me know that my husband had an apostolic calling on his life from his birth. The devil, being aware of his destiny, had made many unsuccessful attempts to kill and destroy him through the years.

Father God let me know that He had bestowed wisdom and ability far beyond Howard's formal education and his age, for no one else could handle those assignments. Further study of the Word revealed conclusive evidence that the apostle could flow in the ministry of a prophet, evangelist, pastor and teacher.

What an intense delight to see and understand an unmistakable picture of our life and ministry unfold before my eyes. It would be delightful to examine each facet and to show you God's eternal destiny in each assignment, but I will save that for eternity when we have all the time in the world.

The intensity of this revelation remains in effect. I consistently see the tasks God requires of my husband. They continue to be arduous, daunting and formidable. But pleasing God is number one in Howard's life.

The Lord ministered greatly to my spirit and soul and promised me He would allow us to return to the cities where He wanted Howard be a part of establishing the foundational New Testament leadership in large congregations. At one point, three of these churches were in the top 100 in attendance for their denominations. During later visits to all these churches, the Lord allowed the leadership to acknowledge publicly Howard's contribution to God's blessing on the work there. It was indeed a blessing to understand God's overall design and purpose as our Father performs His work here on earth, using imperfect but yielding vessels.

CHAPTER TWENTY-NINE

✿

Betty's Perspective – The Golden Years

After graduating from high school in 2000, our oldest grandson Matt felt the call of God on his life and entered a Christian university in Costa Mesa, California. During his first semester, Matt was dismayed that not everyone he met was serious concerning ministry. Instead, they were intent on having good times, and partying was their primary motivation. Matt was ready to quit after mid-term. He had an overwhelming desire to go into ministry, but felt he was not progressing at this school.

I had heard about a program for those who were feeling a ministry call, so we encouraged him to go online to check this opportunity. He was so excited and decided to submit applications to the Master's Commission Programs in Oregon and in Sacramento, California. Matt was enthusiastically accepted into the program at Capitol Assembly, and was to be mentored by a woman named Jeanne Mayo. Matt excelled in the program, and Jeanne personally mentored him another year.

When we met Jeanne at Matt's first-year graduation, she asked Howard and me to be her Dad and Mom, as both her parents had passed away and she needed someone to undergird her in prayer. We have remained her spiritual parents through the years, for we all need special intercession when the rough spots come our way.

I truly wish more of the generations following ours would see their need for spiritual fathers and mothers. Over the years, God has placed me in the lives of some very precious young mothers who have expressed their desperate need for mentoring and I am presently asking the Lord to show me the way to continue doing so.

As a part of the Master's Commission Program, Jeanne arranged for Matt to go to a Revival church in Brownsville, Florida, to get more training. Matt also journeyed to The Tabernacle in Atlanta, where he helped Jeanne start a new Master's Commission. When we came through Atlanta in the summer of 2004 and ministered at the church, Jeanne told us she wanted to keep Matt there, but she knew that when the time came she would help him find the will of God.

In summer 2005 she recommended him for the position of Senior and Junior High School pastor for a large Charismatic church in Loveland, Colorado. He accepted the position and, in just a few months, the staff flew Josh, our youngest grandson, out to Colorado and hired him to become the church webmaster and worship leader for the Junior High ministry. Soon Josh also became the church's sound man.

Both boys married girls they met at the Christian high school in Vista, California, and each started his married life in Greeley, Colorado, just a few miles from Loveland. Within a year or so, Cyndi and Dennis decided to move to Colorado. That meant we had no one left in California to handle our business and care for our property while we traveled in the motor home ministry.

So during our 2006 ministry trip in the motor home we stopped in Loveland for two weeks. Dennis and Cyndi had just moved into their beautiful, newly built home in Greeley. Matt and Fawn, who were married in August 2005, were also able to move into a new home in Greeley. Actually, for a long time I had really been wanting to leave California. Now my heart's desire to move was increasingly growing, for the only close ties we had in the San Diego area were Howard's brother Lee, his wife Fran, and their family. Our daughter Sandi and her husband Martin, lived in Montclair, California.

I always cherished our time with these loved ones and knew we would consistently miss them. But for so many years we had tried to find a local church where we could feel connected. We had pastored two churches in the area, but we hadn't kept close ties when we left.

I can't fully explain it, but there seems to be a difference in the way of thinking and attitudes of the general population in California compared to some other parts of our country. As we traveled for 18 years, I steadily longed to be surrounded with warmth, sincerity and genuine acceptance. This had become my overwhelming desire and I have no doubt the Lord had instilled this in my heart. I just couldn't suppress it. In addition, sound reasoning told me my only two grandsons, whom I have always cherished, would soon be presenting us with great-grandchildren and I really wanted to be an integral part of their lives.

My precious husband and best friend knew well all my thoughts and desires. But Howard pointed out that we had financial stability in California, and certainly the best weather and climate anyone could hope for! If we left California, Howard actually preferred the Dallas-Fort Worth area. Plus, he hated the idea of moving again at our age. He often reminded me of my very words when we left Michigan and moved to California in 1963, "Honey, don't ever take me back to cold county!"

When we visited Colorado, everyone told us the winters were very mild. One of the realtors who showed us property told us her son was 13 years old and had never had enough snow to make a snowman in their yard. But Howard wasn't impressed. He grew up in Nebraska and remembered the abundant snow in the western part of that state and on the eastern plains of Colorado. He remembered winters so brutal that cattle were lost, frozen and covered with snow.

Finally though, Howard agreed to move. He told me, "You have moved so many times and followed me all over the world. It's time I gave in to your heart's desire."

Earlier that year, I had received a prophetic word from a genuine servant of the Lord. "You think your ministry is about over," she related. "No, no, no! Be restored from your heartaches, hurts and weariness, for there will be a new commissioned field of harvest before you."

She proceeded to minister to others, then returned to me saying, "The word I gave you, I hope you hear it and can see it. There's so much ahead for you. Stop struggling and enter into what God has appointed for you at this time in your life. For it will happen soon!"

There were no doubts in my mind that this Colorado move was in God's divine plan for our lives. Together, we made the decision to select a piece of property, find a builder and choose our new model home to be completed before the end of the year.

We felt we should keep all our commitments to attend meetings in Indiana, Mississippi, Louisiana, Oklahoma and Arizona before going home to put our house in California up for sale. However, when we arrived home, we were faced with the reality that property values in our area were falling thousands of dollars each week. Selling this home became one of the greatest demonic battles of our lives. The enemy challenged this decision beyond our comprehension.

Remember, when God reveals a pivotal **plan** for your life, immediately the devil has a stupendous **plot** to hinder, manipulate, bog down, hold back progress, put up barriers, create obstacles, cripple and make you weak so you will reject and discard God's perfect plan.

The Lord revealed to me many years ago that according to the Word of God, the devil is not a **warrior**. Truth in the Word tells us God is the mighty man of war and He is teaching our fingers to fight. He has given us all the weapons necessary to come against our enemy, who has already been defeated. From July 2006 until April 1, 2007, I arose each day between two and four in the morning and, until 7 a.m., I worked against the enemy's plot by engaging all the weapons of warfare granted to me in the Word of God.

The Lord gave me this word: "I am preparing you to enter into a new realm of my power and glory as a priest, for I desire that you rise up as my instrument in this time of turbulence and crisis. Discipline your spirit to intercede. Meditate and hear my spiritual strategic battle plan. I will put the scepter of Miriam, Deborah and Esther in your hand and you will go forward in power and authority and **destroy** the **enemy** before you."

So I began to play songs of praise and to sing and dance before the Lord, as Miriam. I battled against the enemy as Deborah, expecting the stars (the angelic warring forces) to join me in their courses just as she did. I bravely took the stand as Esther did, even if it required my total being. Because the enemy's plot would be defeated.

On a Sunday in October, our anniversary, the Lord spoke to my spirit, saying, "Your spiritual brook has dried up in California and New Life ministries cease to flow in this state."

The Lord let me know He was moving us to Colorado, where the oil of the Spirit would flow, and fresh bread from heaven would be available to feed many. In addition, He said our ministry home would be a haven for the weary and hurting, and the apostolic and prophetic anointing would increase to new levels. The glory of the Lord was coming upon us in a way we hadn't previously known. He let me know the years of experiences and the seeds we had sown in difficult assignments and places would begin to bring forth fruit.

What a challenge to continue my warfare against our raging enemies! But I had God's indisputable promises to me that I could hold up before Him.

While in prayer one day I heard, "Because Howard has honored my 10 Commandments and has displayed them on your property for the world to see, I will honor the 'For Sale by Owner' sign that you have placed on your property. The time will come when I will bring the perfect buyer for your home."

At this time we were tied up with a realtor who had absolutely no interest in selling our home and would not let us out of the year-long contract under which we had been placed without our permission. This contract would bind us until July 2007.

While in prayer and warfare, the Lord then told me we were being positioned for the opportune moment when the sovereignty of God in our lives would line up with our destiny. This has been God's eternal plan since before our births. Again, we were brought face to face with understanding God's timing.

This certainly was not a new experience for us. I had taught on this subject many times and was inspired by the Holy Spirit to write a song on the subject of "Our Father God's Clock." Here we were again in the middle of another golden trial, challenging our faith and believing. In the song I acknowledge that God's clock is not the same as ours, for He is in tomorrow now and He never left yesterday and He was and is and evermore shall be. We will never comprehend God's timing until we have our glorified bodies. Then time won't matter anymore.

At this point we were told our property value had fallen $100,000. Meanwhile, our new home was completed around the beginning of December and they began to fine us every day until we came to close escrow. So we made the journey to Windsor, Colorado a few days before Christmas.

Of course, the day after signing escrow, the largest blizzard in years hit the area and kept us in Dennis and Cyndi's home for over two days. Howard's forecast of eastern Colorado weather was right on and I came face to face with the reality concerning Colorado weather. Even so, it had no effect on my decision to claim this state as my home. We had a wonderful time together with our family and were so happy to celebrate Josh and Andrea's engagement and to look forward to their wedding in April.

Once we managed to free ourselves from the snow and get back to California, the enemy opposition continued fierce and heavy. But the weapons at my disposal were mighty. For many hours each day I used my unbounded patience and perseverance in my office of a priest.

In March 2007, we accepted an offer on the property made by another realtor and we made the decision to move the first of April. Cyndi and Dennis flew out and helped us get all our belongings ready for the moving company. It was a monumental task at our age, but God enabled us to bid goodbye to California on schedule.

Howard drove the packed motor home and pulled the loaded-down Hyundai. Dennis and Cyndi took turns driving the '91 Lincoln Town Car, which was packed to the limit. Not many miles had passed, however, when we got a phone call informing us the sale of our property had fallen out of escrow. My heart may have skipped a few beats, but up in my spirit came God's promise: "The home will be sold by owner and you will have no commissions to pay." Soon after, a couple contacted us to rent the property temporarily, with an agreement that the property would remained for sale.

On April 3, we moved into our beautiful Windsor, Colorado home, just a few miles north of the church where our family was in ministry. We were so thankful to be able to be there for Josh and Andrea's wedding in mid-April.

"So," you may ask, "did everything fall into line and did perfect happiness rule once we arrived in God's promised place?"

No. Remember this fact: the enemy always has a plot when God has established a plan for your life. This was certainly true for us. There were over a hundred significant issues we encountered with the house. We exerted months of patience and pressure on builders and contractors in order to correct their mistakes and blunders.

Also, at 79 years old, Howard decided to become his own landscaper. He hired a man part-time, alongside whom he could work and use his own creative gift in that area. Once more in his life, months of dedicated hard work were required of him, but the result was a park-like setting of breathless natural beauty.

In October 2007, we made our last ministry tour in the motor home. We drove to Indiana for several services and to visit my mother and my brothers in Kokomo. My mother was in her nineties and was becoming frail. It was comforting to me to know we were closer now to my family in Indiana. During this trip, several factors came up that made us both aware that our motor home ministry had come to an end.

Despite the price of diesel fuel, the financial crunch the country was experiencing, and the fact that motor home factories and distributors were going broke from lack of demand, the Lord allowed us to find a buyer for ours. Dealers told us we lucked out, but we told them our Lord was in charge and His abundant favor never failed us.

While in Indiana, we had the chance to minister in Kokomo and in Gary at that first church we pastored and which Howard built in 1952. My mother's health was deteriorating and it was unbelievably difficult to leave her, for I knew it would be the last time I would see her on this earth. In fact, she went to be with the Lord just before Mother's Day, 2009, and it was heart-breaking for all our family to let her go. She was nearing 93 years of age and went to her reward with Jesus and my father who has been there since 1988.

After that Indiana trip, toward the end of November 2007, we received word that the tenants had vacated our home in California. Howard went out there to observe what had to be done in order to sell the property. All the family here did not want to see him make major improvements and we sought the Lord for His perfect plan. The day after he arrived, Howard placed the sign in the yard: "For Sale by Owner".

Almost immediately a businessman came by and asked to take a look at the property for his son's family. The next day he brought his wife to see the property and the following day the son and daughter-in-law came. On the fourth day we had an offer.

We had come to realize the property was not going to sell for the original asking price as all California prices had been inflated for several years. In reality, few properties were selling in that county and it was devastating to owners who could neither sell nor continue to live in their homes. When Howard called me about the proposed sale, it did not take long for us to realize God had sent this buyer, especially since he was offering **cash**! We rejoiced in the mighty hand of God working on our behalf, for escrow closed in three days – another unheard-of situation. How we all rejoiced and I realized again that God's timing is perfect!

In Colorado, we felt accepted by some very dear neighbors and by the precious body of Christ in the area. Howard has ministered in numerous area churches for special services. He has filled in for pastors and ministered at revival services. Even with this schedule, we are able to attend our home church on Saturday evenings. (They also have two Sunday morning services to accommodate all those who attend.) The Lord let Howard know early on that He wanted us to attend a number of churches here in Northern Colorado and declare and prophesy a great outpouring of His Spirit and that a great revival is coming to this area. Consequently, we go to a Sunday morning service wherever the Lord leads us.

We found that many congregations to which we were led were quite dead, and others were hungry for the move of the Spirit. The Lord continues to use Howard consistently to prophesy life, encouragement and exhortation to churches in our area and north to Cheyenne, Wyoming.

In November 2007 he was in the pulpit for some 20 to 30 minutes, prophesying that revival and many supernatural miracles of God were coming to our large home church congregation in Loveland. He prophesied that the revival would spread from Denver, north to Cheyenne and from the west mountain range to the eastern plains of Colorado. Within a few months, this outpouring came to our church and is still continuing in powerful healings, signs and wonders. People are being drawn in to this church in a phenomenal way.

Our beloved pastor of 32 years retired this past July. He had been patiently anticipating this move of God and for his successor as pastor. On that November night, in the same prophecy, the Holy Spirit declared the next Worship and Arts Pastor whom He would send would be as cream rising to the top of milk.

After the new Worship and Arts Pastor arrived, we all knew he was a man sent from God. He maintained that he just wanted to be Worship and Arts Pastor, but God gave Howard a word for him, indicating that he would be a Senior Pastor. Not long after, he consented to preach and our pastor knew without doubt that God had sent his replacement. It warmed our hearts to hear our Pastor Emeritus say to Howard that the church has not been the same since God sent us here.

On Sunday evenings, God has also used us to consistently attend and help in the ministry at a Full Gospel church in Greeley. We are not on staff, but they give us gifts for Christmas and Pastor Appreciation Day and I am so blessed to play the organ there every Sunday evening. Howard weekly attends the 6:33 men's ministry and the intercessory prayer on Thursday mornings at our home church. I attend the Women's Rapha Bible Study and enjoy being a prayer counselor for their monthly meetings and yearly advances. I was so privileged and it was a joy to my heart to fill in for the Senior Bible Study teacher who was unable to teach from September to April this past year.

Howard and I have not shared all these details with you to exalt ourselves, but only to give glory to our Heavenly Father who has called us and allowed us to be vessels used to perpetuate His Kingdom even in our golden years. We so desire that our lives and experiences will bring to you much encouragement, a greater faith, new hope and renewed trust in our Lord. We give him all the Glory!

Before I come to the end of my contribution to this book, I must tell you my first great-granddaughter, Riley Kate, came into this world on December 31, 2009, born to Matt and Fawn. She is a beauty and has brought incredible joy to our family. On August 11, 2010, Madison Brooke was born to Josh and Andrea. She is another grand prize! They both are the sweetest, smartest and most photogenic children we have ever known. (Just go on their mothers' Facebook pages and you will have to agree.) What a blessing they are!

This past October 1 was our 60th Anniversary. The following Sunday, Cyndi and Dennis and the family gave us an anniversary party that surpassed all others. It was held in the high school auditorium at our church and there were almost 400 who attended! We were overwhelmed with the beautiful decorations, with all the people who love us, with the food and beautiful donated cake, and with the program that included a video and CD of our life and ministry together.

One time, in the late '80s, as I was preparing a Wednesday night Bible study, the Lord stirred my heart to understand about His grace in a more specific manner. I titled my presentation, "My Friend, Grace!" And, during our eighteen-year motor home ministry, I often found myself sharing on this subject. More revelation constantly came to me on this topic. I began to see the vastness of His grace, which is so much more than amazing and more than unmerited favor as the Amplified Bible translates.

In January 1990, I was inspired to write: "In **grace** are three concepts: #1 the **divine influence** in our lives as Christians, which enables us to stand strong and live an overcoming life. #2 the **divine resources** available to us; power, authority, healing the sick and deliverance from any occasion which arises against us. #3 the **divine ability** given to enable us to accomplish the calling God has given us."

Before our pastor John retired, he shared in a series of messages that grace is not just unmerited favor of God, but is the divine influence in our lives, helping us to keep free from sin. I almost jumped out of my seat when he said this for I had not heard this teaching from anyone else before. During the last year, while in study and prayer, I began to realize that, in grace's **divine influence** is the seedbed for the nine fruits of the Spirit in Galatians 5; which are to grow in our lives as Christians.

In Grace's **divine resources** is the reception area for the nine gifts of the Spirit available to the Spirit-filled body of Christ, which will operate in our lives according to I Corinthians 12.

In Grace's **divine ability** is the capacity to accomplish God's call and destiny for our lives. There is a power base for the fivefold ministry in Ephesians 4:11 and 12 and the seven motivational gifts in Romans 12:7 and 8.

If you relate to these concepts of grace, I trust you will study the scriptures given and many others on this subject. Since I grasped hold of the truths of **grace**, realizing all these three concepts are **supernatural** and **unlimited**, it has tremendously enriched my life. So I trust all who read these words may understand the full measure of **grace** in your life. "For all things are for your sakes, that the abundant grace might through the thanksgiving of many redound to the glory of God." II Corinthians 4:15.

It is our desire that, through reading this book, you will be inspired to join us on this **supernatural walk**, for it will be a vital requirement in these last troublesome days. You will enjoy freedom, joy and a new intimacy with the Lord and be prepared for this mighty army of believers who receives an impartation of His sovereign power. Remember, as Howard shares prophetic words in the last chapter of this book, "The future for the Church is as bright as the promises of God."

CHAPTER THIRTY

✥

The Future for the Church is as Bright as the Promises of God

I prophesy that there is a great storm coming to America and to the world. The events that happen will be absolutely unbelievable. There will be desolation, chaos and confusion in America. We are going to see riots, men and women moving about as packs of dogs, murdering, thieving, destroying and committing all kinds of evil things. There is going to be disruption and disorder and multitudes of Christians will be disillusioned. I see in the Spirit such anarchy, chaos and devastation coming. This will be the notable opportunity that God has planned for the church. So prepare and be ready.

There will need to be those who have been tested, tried and proven so they might be empowered by the Spirit to bring life. Remember when God sent the prophet Ezekiel to speak to the bone yard. As he began to prophesy and speak life into those dead, dry bones, they began to shake and come alive. The prophetic word has power and life. God wants to use you in the prophetic. For the Word says covet to prophesy.

If the Holy Spirit anoints you, it brings life. I have seen it over and over and over! I've seen the devil dispelled and cast out. Many great things have been accomplished because of the prophetic word I have spoken. Ezekiel's bone yard came alive with the spoken word. They stood upright and became a great army. Likewise, God is raising up a great army today in the power and might of the Spirit of the Lord. He wants us to realize that it is not by might nor by power alone, but by His Spirit.

The Spirit of the Lord is going to come upon those who are looking for His enablement as never before. For the scripture says, "The yoke will be destroyed because of the anointing."

An anointing is coming upon the body of Christ greater than any before, and they will walk in the **supernatural** in a deeper, fuller and more powerful and complete way. From the whole body, God is preparing a people who are after His heart and desirous to do His will. And they will be those who will minister to the many disillusioned Christians.

Many pastors have allowed churches to remain lukewarm or cold. They have not taught the truth and have not prepared their people for this day. It is the beginning of sorrows, but God is going to bring us through, victorious in whatever we face, as we trust in Him.

So be strong and be of good courage. This is the Word of the Lord to you now, just as He said it to Joshua who was to lead the children of Israel over the Jordan River and into the promise land. The Holy Spirit is saying now to us, "Don't be afraid. Be of good courage and be strong, for Jesus has overcome the wicked one and already gotten you the victory. Therefore you are able to do more than you could ask or think."

Trust Him with all your heart. Lean not to your own understanding. Be radical in faith and go forth in the power and the might of the Spirit of God. The Lord will go before you and prepare the way. For you have power over all the power of the enemy and nothing by any means shall hurt you. Even though you may be in the fire, the flood or the lion's den, the Lord is with you and He is strengthening you to come out strong and mighty.

The Holy Spirit is saying, "You can be just like Daniel, whom the lions didn't touch or even scratch. And you can be just like Shadrach, Meshach and Abednego who came out of that fiery furnace, heated seven times hotter, and did not have the smell of smoke on them."

For the Lord says you will come through this fire, through this flood and through the lion's den and be strong and courageous. So know that it is your faith that is being tried. You are being toughened so that you will be a strong soldier for Jesus Christ. You must endure hardness for it makes no difference how difficult or how great the problem may be. It's not worthy to compare with the glory that is prepared for those who will diligently follow the Lord. The day of the Lord is near at hand. The time is far spent. The day cometh when no man can work.

It is time to go forward in the name of the Lord conquering, for He is teaching you to walk totally with Him in the **supernatural**. Remember, you are not only a natural man, but as a born again Christian and believer in the Lord Jesus Christ, you are also supernatural. You can rise up and do great and mighty exploits in his name.

Use His name, use His word and go forth. For the Lord is with you. He delights in destroying the enemy. Since you have already gotten the victory through Jesus Christ, nothing that you face can destroy you. Rise up in faith knowing that God has given you power and authority over all the power of the enemy. In everything you face, you have power, strength and ability to overcome. It is by your faith that God will make you more than a conqueror.

I believe very soon we are going to be released and a new anointing is coming. There will be meetings where everyone present will be healed. God is going to pour out His love, His mercy, His compassion, and the gifts of the Spirit are going to flow so freely. Yes, God is going to show forth His mercy, His goodness and His love just before the great outpouring of the wrath of God that is coming upon this world, which was spoken by the prophets Ezekiel, Daniel and John.

Be ready and prepare yourself, for the day of the Lord is coming. Great anarchy is coming in the United States and in the world.

Everything that can be shaken is going to be shaken, the Lord says. If we are in the Kingdom of God, we can't be shaken. We are in that Kingdom of righteousness, peace and joy in the Holy Ghost.

Scores will wonder what to do. But we will have the answers, not the government. For God is going to use the Church, the body of Christ. I want to emphasize that the whole body will be involved; and there will be many who have never been used before. God is preparing you. This is why you are going through these situations you do not understand. Hold steady, my child, and be ready to be used of the Lord. For He is preparing you to be the solution to the problem. God is preparing to pour out an anointing about which we know nothing at this moment. He will endue us with His power and enable us.

I encourage you to stand steadfast and immovable, knowing that your God has everything under control and He is going to bring victory through you. The time will come when many churches will have to remain open 24/7, because there will be so many disillusioned people searching for answers and asking for help. Praise God, the body of Christ are the ones who will have the answers to the problems. Since the foundation of the world, God has been preparing a people for this time. He will enable you and give you wisdom, knowledge, ability and power to minister to those He brings to you. It will be far beyond our comprehension, for it will be the Spirit of God as He will begin to move us into the **supernatural** and we will become different people.

God's angels are going to become more and more involved in the ministry that God assigns. Through us the Lord will bring forth miracles, signs and wonders and angelic hosts are going to help us and minister with us in a greater way.

The Bible says in the 91st Psalm, "He will give His angels charge over thee; to keep thee in all thy ways."

The Lord is going to give us greater protection and greater authority; therefore the angels of the Lord are going to be involved in a greater way in our lives and ministry. The Lord teaches us in Revelations 12:12, "...

For the devil is come down unto you, having great wrath, because he knoweth that he hath but a short time."

The Lord has promised in Romans 9:28, "For He will finish the work and cut it short in righteousness, because a short work will the Lord make upon the earth."

So we need to be ready for what God is about to do, for it will be the greatest outpouring and manifestation of God's power. It will be the greatest war between God and Satan. But we know who wins because we've read the back of the book!

God is going to use you and me: the body of Christ. It will be a short work, a powerful work, and angelic hosts are going to be involved in our lives as we minister and go forth in this increased anointing of the Holy Spirit. We just need to be courageous and be strong. For the Lord is going to be by our side every moment of every day and He will never leave us or forsake us.

The Bible teaches in 1 Kings 19:58 how the angels minister **to** us. Elijah had just won a great victory. But then he found himself in the desert, needing encouragement. The Lord sent an angel who baked him a cake and ministered **to** him on two occasions. And he went in the strength of that meal prepared by the angel.

God used angels to minister **to** Jesus in Matthew 4:11, in the great trial of His faith during the time of fasting and prayer prior to going into the ministry that God ordained for Him.

In Hebrews 1:14 it reads, "Are they not all ministering Spirits sent forth to minister **for** them who shall be the heirs of salvation?"

In Acts 12:5-11, angels were sent to open the gates for God's ministers.

I say to you that God is about to do a new thing and bring forth what He has planned this day from the foundations of the earth and He is going to use us.

I have walked forward in faith at times. As I shared earlier in this book, God sent an angel to help me build the church when I was an inexperienced young man in the ministry in Gary, Indiana. God will truly help us if we will trust and depend upon Him.

When I was pastoring the church in Redlands, California, the Lord revealed to me that He was calling us into traveling ministry. We were to go into the entire world and never ask for meetings and never ask for finances or solicit funds in any way.

I said, "God, how can I do this? I don't understand how this can happen and I don't know what to do."

The Lord spoke to me and said, "Don't you remember when you were building the church in Gary? I helped you and I sent my angel to help you. You didn't know what to do, but I knew. For I have your future planned and I will help you now and send my angel to assist you even as I did before."

I began to rise up with good courage and faith, for as I looked back at what He had done, I knew He was also well able to take care of the future.

After the Lord shared with me that He had sent his angel to help me build that church, Betty and I were in the worship service of a large church. The pastor suddenly stopped preaching and said, "Howard, there are two of the biggest angels standing on either side of you. They are about nine feet tall and nobody should ever bother you, for God has you protected."

I have never seen them but I believe the angels of the Lord are with me because He promised they would be sent to take charge over us.

In the Word of God, there are many occasions when God sent angels and it was obvious that angels were involved in the protection, blessing and helping in ministry and leadership of those who followed Him. On other occasions there have been those who reported to me they saw angels beside me and behind me when I was ministering. I did not see them, but I believe they were there and I was expecting them to help me, for I need all the help I can get!

One time I was ministering at a convention in Mississippi. After the meeting, a man told me he saw Jesus standing by my right side. He said that Jesus would whisper things into my ear and then I would speak forth in Words of Knowledge and prophetic utterances. God was doing great things in that convention.

We need to prepare ourselves to expect Jesus, the head of the church, and the angelic hosts to help us in our ministry in a more profound way. The Bible teaches us in Hebrews 13:9 "Be not forgetful to entertain strangers for thereof some have entertained angels unaware."

We are not to worship angels, but we may entertain them. Praise God the Lord is going to do a quick work and the devil knows that his time is short as we learn in Revelations. He is doing all he can do. The war is going to intensify; but we win and just need to stay in faith, believing that God will bring to pass those things He promised and that He will enable us as we put our total confidence and trust in Him.

So hallelujah! Rise up in faith and face the enemy. The Lord has given you power over all the power of the enemy and nothing by any means will hurt you. **You can stand on it. You can bank on it. For God surely will bring to pass great things in these last days. So expect great anointings to fall upon you. For it is not you, but the Holy Spirit to whom you are yielding who is doing these works through you. And out of your belly shall flow rivers of living water, and this is the power of the Holy Spirit.** In this river are all the gifts of the Spirit, the ability to cast out devils and to do whatever God calls you to do. Because the Holy Spirit will enable you.

So go forth in Jesus' name and know that no weapon formed against you will prosper, for the Lord is with you. It is His ministry operating through you.

Therefore, be His mouthpiece, His eyes, His ears, His hands and His feet and be bold in the Lord and be very courageous for the great and mighty things the Lord is going to do through you. We must remember it is the Lord Jesus Christ who is accomplishing His purpose though us. Let go of all the things of this world. Become more like Jesus, remain humble, give Him all the glory, honor and praise and He will flow through you in a greater way.

The Lord is telling me that the reason this particular period of time shall be a quick and short work is so no one will be able to say, I did this or I did that. For He will not allow any person to build a ministry on the astronomical great signs and wonders or take the credit for what He will be doing. The Lord will receive all the glory, for it belongs to Him. We must practice Proverbs 3:5, "Trust in the Lord with all your heart, with all your soul, with all your strength, with every thing that is within you and lean not to your own understanding." The promise is: the Lord will provide. Remember, when the Lord gives vision, He gives provision. For **He is our provision – a mighty army going forth**.

I give Him glory, honor and praise for that which He is doing. I believe He is getting the body of Christ ready all over the world and He has shown me that He is preparing us to go forth in His name like a mighty army all over the world. In the United States, He is preparing an army of people that will rise up in His strength and His ability and will go forth doing miracles. And there will be signs and wonders.

It is going to be very easy; we will be surprised and astounded with what God is going to do through us. He already is doing wonderful things, but it is going to accelerate to a greater degree. I thank God that not only here in America is He preparing a people for a mighty army, but all over the world. It seems everywhere we go there are people upon whom God is putting His greater anointing. His anointing is going to increase exceedingly. But until then we will go through difficult times, severe testing and trials to prove us and to cause us to be extremely strong when the Lord sends us out into the battlefield.

So look up to the Lord and know that He will use you if you will prepare yourself in prayer, fasting and studying the word. Grow in grace and the knowledge of Jesus Christ. Greater things are to come and He is the one who is going to do it. Give Him glory and Honor.

We had a wonderful time in China, seeing those beautiful people and how they loved Jesus Christ. We saw how they worshiped, how they praised and how they longed to be taught the word and to be endued with His power. Let it be so with us in whom God is going to do a new thing. He is going to do it. The Lord is calling His church to disembark the cruise ship and board the battleship!

"Lift up your heads, O you gates! And be lifted up, you everlasting doors! And the King of glory shall come in. Who is this King of glory? The Lord strong and mighty, the Lord mighty in battle." Psalms 24: 7 and 8

"Through God we will do valiantly. For it is He who shall tread down our enemies." Psalms 60:12

"Let the high praises of God be in their mouth, and a two-edged sword in their hand, to execute vengeance on the nations and punishments on the peoples; To bind their kings with chains, and their nobles with fetters of iron; To execute on them the written judgment – This honor have all His saints. Praise the Lord!" Psalm 149:6-9

"But if you indeed obey His voice and do all that I speak, then I will be an enemy to your enemies and an adversary to your adversaries." Exodus 23:22

"You will chase your enemies, and they shall fall by the sword before you. Five of you shall chase a hundred, and a hundred of you shall put ten thousand to flight." Leviticus 26:7 and 8

"But thanks be to God, who gives us the victory through our Lord Jesus Christ. Therefore, my beloved brethren, be steadfast, immovable, always abounding in the work of the Lord, knowing that your labor is not in vain in the Lord." I Corinthians 15:57

"You are of God, little children, and have overcome them, because He who is in you is greater than he who is in the world." I John 5:4

"And there shall be signs in the sun, and in the moon, and in the stars; and upon the earth distress of nations, with perplexity; the sea and the waves roaring; Men's hearts failing them for fear, and for looking after those things which are coming on the earth; for the powers of heaven shall be shaken. And then shall they see the Son of man coming in a cloud with power and great glory. And when these things begin to come to pass, then look up, and lift up your heads; for your redemption draweth nigh." Luke 21:25-28

"For as the lightning cometh out of the east, and shineth even unto the west; so shall also the coming of the Son of man be." Matthew 24:27

"Henceforth there is laid up for me a crown of righteousness, which the Lord, the righteous judge, shall give me at that day: and not to me only, but unto all them also that loves his appearing." I Timothy 4:8

"Looking for that blessed hope, and the glorious appearing of the great God and our Savior Jesus Christ." Titus 2:13

Keep pressing toward the mark! "I press toward the mark for the prize of the high calling of God in Christ Jesus." Philippians 4:14

"Fight the good fight of faith, lay hold on eternal life, where unto thou art also called, and hast professed a good profession before many witnesses." I Timothy 6:12

Then one day you will hear the sweetest words said to you by Jesus:

"His Lord said unto him, well done, thou good and faithful servant; thou hast been faithful over a few things, I will make thee ruler over many things; enter thou into the joy of thy Lord." Matthew 25:21

About the Authors

Howard and Betty Skinner were married October 1, 1950. They have two daughters, two grandsons and two great-granddaughters. In the fall of 1951 they entered full-time ministry after serving faithfully in part-time ministry. They are seasoned ministers having pastored a total of eight churches from Indiana, Michigan and California. They have traveled around the world in Missionary Evangelism in about twenty-five countries and have ministered in most of the fifty states. They currently reside in Windsor, Colorado.